House Painting

Created and Designed by the Editorial Staff of Ortho Books

Project Editor
Jill Fox

Writers
Topcoat Painters
(Mark Terwilliger
Joseph Lavenia)

Illustrator
Mitzi McCarthy

Photo Editor
Roberta Spieckerman

Principal Photographer
Kenneth Rice

Ortho Books

Publisher
Richard E. Pile, Jr.

Editorial Director
Christine Jordan

Production Director
Ernie S. Tasaki

Managing Editors
Robert J. Beckstrom
Michael D. Smith
Sally W. Smith

System Manager
Linda M. Bouchard

Marketing Specialist
Daniel Stage

Sales Manager
Thomas J. Leahy

Distribution Specialist
Barbara F. Steadham

Technical Consultant
J. A. Crozier, Jr., Ph.D.

Address all inquiries to:
Ortho Books
Chevron Chemical Company
Consumer Products Division
Box 5047
San Ramon, CA 94583-0947

Copyright © 1992
Chevron Chemical Company
All rights reserved under international and Pan-American copyright conventions.

2 3 4 5 6 7 8 9
92 93 94 95 96 97 98

ISBN 0-89721-246-0
Library of Congress Catalog Card
Number 92-70584

Editorial Coordinator
Cass Dempsey

Copyeditor
Irene Elmer

Proofreader
Deborah Bruner

Indexer
Patricia Feuerstein

Editorial Assistant
John Parr

Composition by
Laurie A. Steele

Production by
Studio 165

Separations by
Color Tech Corp.

Lithographed in the USA by
Webcrafters, Inc.

Consultants and Painters
Names of consultants and painters are followed by the page numbers on which their work appears.

Bob Buckter Color Consulting; San Francisco: 6, 28, 40L
Decorative Painting & Ornament Co.; Sonoma, Calif.: 3B, 76–77
Michael Deenikan Painting; Sonoma, Calif.: 3B, 76–77
Tony Enenich Painting; Newark, Calif.: 74
Kurtz Painting Company; Albany, Calif.: 95
O'Brien Painted to Last; Berkeley, Calif.: 32, 78
Orlando Trujillo Painting; San Mateo, Calif.: 6
Judy Jones Salerno/Color Consultant; Santa Rosa, Calif.: 33
John Salerno Drywall and Painting; Santa Rosa, Calif.: 33
Topcoat Painters; Berkeley, Calif.: 4–5

Special Thanks to
David Allswang
Buckter family
Marie Cleasby
Dunlop family
Kip & Susan Edenborough
Richard J. Fateman
John Fleming
Scott Graham
Bonnie Heedlee, Trades Guild
Rosemarie Indelicato
Jacobson family
Maddox family
Keith Pyburn
Robert E. Scott
Terry Southworth
Wakeman family
Mike and Mary Weiland, East Bay Paint Center

Photographers
Names of photographers are followed by the page numbers on which their work appears.
R = right, C = center,
L = left, T = top, B = bottom.

Russell Abraham: 38B, 41T
Benjamin Moore Paint Company: 7, 98
Laurie A. Black: 8T, 25, 47
Hedrich Blessing: 26–27
The Color People: 8B, 21, 35T, 43, 52, 93
Barbara J. Ferguson: 19B, 109TR
Michael Garland: 49, 103, 109B
Susan M. Lammers: 101B
Michael McKinley: 34T, 109TL
K. Micalchuck: 38T
National Paint & Coatings Association: 34B, 35B, back cover TL, back cover BR
Geoff Nilsen: 13, 19T
Said Nuseibeh: 91
The O'Brien Corporation/Fuller O'Brien Paints: 3T, 14, 40R
Ortho Library: 36B, 108
Kenneth Rice: front cover, title page, 3B, 4–5, 6, 28, 32, 33, 36T, 37, 40T, 41B, 42, 50–51, 53, 54–56, 74, 76–77, 78, 80, 89, 95
Samuel Cabot, Inc.: 9, 20, 44, 45, 46, 69, 100 101T

Front Cover
One way to choose colors for a house is to use those that are historically accurate. The subtle pallet applied to this classic Georgian Revival house reflects the style in which these houses were originally painted.

Title Page
Accentuate the entrance by painting the front door a color in high contrast to the rest of the house. A red door on a blue-toned house is a popular choice.

Page 3
Top: Rich colors emphasize the rich details of this period home.
Bottom: A palette of sunny, warm colors lends an almost tropical look to this country Victorian.

Back Cover
Top left: An appropriate color scheme is one that suits the house and its environment. An analogous scheme allows the garden to stand out.
Top right and bottom left: Colorful illustrations throughout this book provide technical guidance for all stages of painting a house.
Bottom right: In the 1970s the fanciful gingerbread of Victorians inspired the use of multiple trim colors. Today it is used on many house styles.

Chevron Chemical Company
6001 Bollinger Canyon Road, San Ramon, CA 94583

House Painting

Planning the Project

Choosing Colors

Preparation

Painting and Staining

PLANNING THE PROJECT

Houses are painted to define an architectural style, increase the resale value, protect the structure, improve the neighborhood, and please the inhabitants. Good planning is essential for a house-painting project to go well. This chapter explains how to estimate time, materials, equipment needs, and access requirements accurately—important information, whether you intend to do all the work yourself or to hire a contractor.

A good paint job, like the one on this craftsman bungalow, involves planning a color scheme, preparing the surface, choosing top-quality materials, and doing the work well.

ELEMENTS OF A GOOD PAINT JOB

A good paint job looks good and does a good job of protecting the house. The odds are high that your house will be attractive for many years if you choose the colors carefully, prepare the surface well, use high-quality materials, and apply the paint correctly. Having a well-painted house is a matter of performing a series of tasks in the proper order.

Well-Planned Design

A fresh coat of paint makes any house more appealing. A well-planned design brings out the most attractive features of the architecture. Use colors and finishes to highlight interesting areas and hide unattractive features. A design doesn't have to be complex to be effective. The best color scheme is simple, pleasing in itself, and harmonious with its surroundings. It takes into account the style of the house and the colors and shapes around it to make a pleasing overall impression.

Few things that a homeowner can do will improve the appearance of the house for as little effort and expense as a new paint job.

Proper Preparation

Preparation is the most important factor in determining how long a paint job will last. If the existing paint is sound and the desire is only to change the colors, very little preparation may be needed. If the weather has begun to deteriorate the surface of the old paint, it will take some work to make that surface sound before you apply new paint. If the old paint has been left to deteriorate to the point where it is no longer firmly attached to the house, there will be a substantial amount of work to do prior to painting.

Surface preparation is related to the finished appearance of the paint job. The color and the gloss level of the finish coat paint can be used

Highlight unique architectural features, such as the eyebrows over the front windows of this Mediterranean house, by painting them with an accent color.

to de-emphasize rough surface areas. This is a consideration in choosing materials.

Top-Quality Materials

Always buy the best materials you can afford. This is one of the best investments you can make for your house. If you buy cheap materials, you may save a few dollars per gallon, but the paint job will almost certainly deteriorate faster, and in some cases, it may require more preparation and be more difficult to paint in the future. In addition, better-quality paints are often easier to use than inexpensive ones.

Most manufacturers make their paints, and some of their other coatings, in a range of qualities. The top grade of paint from any reputable manufacturer is certainly at least adequate for your needs. The second lines of the better manufacturers are also quite good. The main difference between the top line and the second lines usually lies in the type and amount of vehicle (see page 78). The better paints contain more expensive vehicles, which helps to ensure a tougher, more durable protective coat of paint.

Check *Consumer Reports*, available in most public libraries, for a good current guide to paint qualities. Local painting

Different building materials may require different products. Know the requirements of your particular type of siding before you shop for paint. This Victorian is finished with horizontal board siding.

Right: Picture windows lend themselves to framing. Combine two colors around windows using the same principles as you would use in matting and framing a piece of art.
Bottom: Three accent colors bring out the details of these columns. It takes slightly more masking time, and about 10 percent more painting time, to paint trim in more than one color.

contractors are another good source of information. Though each may have a favorite brand, all should be aware of the relative qualities of locally available products.

Proper Execution

Understanding and using the techniques outlined in this book will ensure that your house will be properly painted. None of the techniques is difficult to master. The most important requirement is that you take the time to perform each task to the best of your ability.

A good paint job is a safe paint job. Working with chemicals, using power tools, and, above all, working from ladders and scaffolding must be done with a proper respect for your life and the laws of physics. It takes no extra time to

be safe; it takes only attention. You must learn and follow the safety precautions in every phase of the work. When it is done properly, painting is not dangerous. What is dangerous is carelessness.

A good paint job is neat and clean, not only in the finished product but also in the work habits of the painter. Of course, preparation and painting can make a dreadful mess—that's half the fun. But clean up as you complete each phase of the job. This makes everything go more smoothly and reduces the chaos to a manageable level.

Chronology of the Job

In tackling a job as big as painting a house, it's a good idea to go through it in your mind and on paper first. Each phase of the job is related to all the other phases. Make the most of your time and effort by identifying problems early. Knowing how much preparation is required helps you to determine what type of paint to use, what levels of gloss to choose, and which features to highlight. The color selection determines the order in which various parts of the house are painted, and so forth.

You will have some latitude in determining the order of the job. You can finish one face of the house completely before starting on the next, or you can do all of the preparation on the whole house first and then all of the painting. However, you must work under a few fixed constraints. The most obvious

is that a surface must be prepared before it is painted. Less obvious is that some kinds of primer must be painted over within a defined period, since they weather quickly when exposed or become too hard to provide a good surface for the next coat of paint.

Each chapter of this book deals with a specific aspect of house painting. The brief chronology given here is an overview—a things-to-do list—of the process as a whole.

1. Inspect the house.

2. Identify the house style and features.

3. List colors of all fixed features, such as roof finish, natural siding, pathways, and landscaping.

4. Identify surface problems.

5. Determine features to highlight or conceal.

6. Choose house body and trim colors.

7. Choose gloss levels best suited to surfaces to be painted.

8. Determine access requirements around the house.

9. Estimate material and equipment needs.

10. Arrange for purchase or rental of tools and equipment.

11. Purchase priming and paint materials.

12. Set up access equipment.

13. Wash the house with water to remove dirt and chalking paint.

14. Use chemicals to kill any mildew; remove the residue.

15. Drop and mask the house appropriately.

16. Remove loose paint from wood and masonry surfaces.

17. Remove loose paint and loose rust from iron and steel and spot-prime the same day with appropriate primer.

18. Smooth the surface by sanding or stripping old paint as necessary.

19. Remove any loose or missing glazing and prepare the bare sash for priming.

20. Identify and make any necessary minor repairs.

21. Spot-prime bare wood.

22. Etch, clean, and prime bare galvanized steel with appropriate primer.

23. Repair window glazing.

24. Patch holes and imperfections, including cracks in stucco and metal.

25. Sand patches smooth and brush away dust.

26. Do all caulking.

27. Apply a full coat of primer, if required. If the next full coat is to be the finish coat, spot-prime patches with the finish material.

28. Apply finish coat to the eaves and overhangs, the house body, the windows, the doors, the other trim and details, the railings, the decks, the thresholds, and finally the steps.

29. Clean painting tools and equipment.

30. Remove and return access equipment.

31. Store and dispose of paint and solvents properly.

Stain does not conceal the beauty of the grain on this horizontal wood siding, nor does it conceal surface problems. Where these are serious consider using paint rather than stain.

Painting Terms

Across the grain   In a piece of wood, across the direction of the natural fibers.

Base coat   The first coat of paint. May refer to a coat that will be visible through subsequent coats, as in graining.

Body   In paint, the consistency of the material.

Box   To mix paint thoroughly by pouring it from one container to another.

Breathe   In dry latex paint, to allow water vapor to pass through without destroying the film.

Bridge   In paint, to span a small gap in the surface over which it is applied.

Brush out   To spread out paint with a brush, usually to an even thickness.

Build   In paint, the thickness of the coat when cured.

Chalk   In paint, to deteriorate, leaving a chalky layer of loose pigment on the surface.

Cross-brush   To smooth out paint by stroking at right angles to the direction in which it will be laid off.

Cut back   To cut in over a previously applied color to define the border between the two colors more sharply.

Cut in   To use a brush to apply paint to an area that cannnot be reached with a roller or a sprayer, or to define the edges of an area.

Drop cloth   A large piece of canvas used to protect nearby surfaces from dust and paint.

Drop off   To cover a work area with drop cloths.

Dry to the touch   The stage when the painted surface is no longer sticky but is not yet completely dry. Sometimes called surface dry or dust free.

Etch   To roughen a smooth surface in preparation for coating, often done by applying chemicals.

Face off   To apply color (usually trim color) to the face only of an object.

Feather out   1. To apply paint or spackling compound in such a way that the film gets thinner and thinner as it approaches the edge of the area coated, until it fades away to nothing. 2. To sand the sharply defined edges of surface imperfections in this same way, tapering them to make them less obvious.

Finish coat   The final decorative and protective coat.

Flashing   A condition of uneven gloss, so called because spots "flash" into view as one looks at the offending area from different angles.

Glaze   1. A semitransparent paint or varnish with some pigment added. 2. To set glass in a window sash. 3. To apply glazing compound to a window sash.

Glaze coat   A layer of semitransparent paint or varnish.

Glazing compound   A high-grade form of putty used to seal glass into place in a window sash.

Grab   In paint, the ability to bond to a surface. Primer applied to a difficult surface is sometimes called a grab coat.

Hold out   In paint and other materials, the ability to seal the surface against stains that come from behind the film.

Holiday   A miss or a blank spot in the coat of paint. Something that should have been painted but wasn't.

House body   The walls of the house, exclusive of openings and decorations.

Lap marks   Visible lines between two areas where paint was applied.

Lay off   To perform the final smoothing with a brush or roller; to make sure that the brush strokes all go in the proper direction and that the roller texture is even.

Lay on   To carry paint from the bucket to the wall and roughly apply it.

Mask   To protect an area from paint by covering it with paper or plastic taped securely in place.

Orange peel   The texture created when tacky paint is rolled over again or when paint is sprayed on too thick.

Overspray   Paint spray that goes where it is not wanted.

Pigment   The coloring agent in paint. By extension, any inert material in paint or stain, including fillers and extenders.

Point   A common unit of measure for pigments and colorants, equal to $\frac{1}{32}$ ounce by volume.

Prime coat   The first layer of a multilayer paint job. It is usually of a different material than the finish coat.

Pull   What tacky paint does when you try to brush it out. Instead of flowing, it forms stringy or rough patterns and feels sticky.

Roller marks   A pattern left on the surface of the paint, usually by excess buildup in the roller.

Roller texture   The pattern left on the surface of the paint by the nap of the roller. An even texture indicates an even film of paint.

Roll on   To apply paint with a roller.

Roll out   To spread paint evenly with a roller.

Run   A river of paint cascading down the wall. Paint runs when it is applied too thick.

Sag   A wide area of paint runs, which produces a rippled effect.

Setup   The collection of tools used together to do a certain job. A roller setup consists of a frame, a sleeve, a tray or a bucket and screen, and, if necessary, a pole.

Soften   To blur the line between two freshly applied colors by mottling it with a brush, usually a soft brush.

Spot-prime   To prime only the areas that need special attention.

Time to recoat   The time from the moment the material is applied to the moment when it can be painted over.

Topcoat   *See* Finish coat.

Touch up   To repair minor defects, such as holidays, by applying more of the same material after the first application is dry.

Trim   All of the decorative elements on the building. Sometimes taken to include doors and windows, as well as their frames.

Vehicle   The medium in paint, stain, and varnish that holds the pigment in suspension and forms the dried film.

Wet edge   The part of a coat of paint that is still wet enough to brush or roll. To keep a wet edge means to paint all of one discrete part of the building without having to brush or roll over either tacky paint or newly dry paint.

Wet on wet   To apply a second coat after the first coat has begun to be absorbed into the surface but before it has had a chance to dry.

With the grain   In a piece of wood, with the direction of the natural fibers. This is usually in line with the long dimension of the piece.

Wood graining   Painting a surface to look like wood.

Working time   The time from the moment when the material is opened, mixed, or made ready for use to the moment when it begins to pull.

Wrap   To carry the face paint color around the edge of an object (usually a piece of trim) and paint the edge in the same color.

ESTIMATING TIME AND MATERIALS

Properly estimating the amount of time needed to paint a house is integral to establishing a proper schedule, whether you do the work yourself or hire it done. Materials must be accurately estimated too. This saves shopping trips, saves you from having to store or return extra paint, and saves you from running out of paint in the middle of the job.

Estimating Time

Estimating how long it will take to prepare and paint a house is a tricky business. Professional painters have estimating standards, but houses vary and a painting job is full of surprises. That said, here are some rules of thumb, which should get you in the right ballpark.

Work up the estimate with pencil and paper, to keep track of details. There is some arithmetic involved, so have a calculator handy. The hours given on pages 12 and 13 represent the time it would take an experienced painter to do a careful job. Expect that it will probably take you longer.

When turning hours into days, remember to include time for setup at the beginning of each session, cleanup at the end of each session, breaks, meals, weather-related interruptions, trips to the store for materials, and time off for good behavior.

Preparation

Estimating time required for preparation is more complex than estimating time required for painting. The rough-and-ready approach is to estimate the preparation time as a multiple of the painting time. If the house is in very good shape and the painting is being done only to change the color, the preparation should take one half or one quarter of the time that it takes to apply one coat of paint. If the house is in good shape overall, but there is a small amount of peeling or deterioration, the preparation should take about the same time as it takes to apply one

coat of paint. If the paint is peeling over a wide area, the estimating process becomes more difficult. If you just want to return to a mechanically sound surface, remove the loose paint, prime, and apply the finish coat, the preparation may take twice as long as it takes to apply one coat of paint. If you want to make the house look like new, the painting could shrink to a small fraction of the total job. In every case, a full prime coat counts as a first coat of paint. Don't include it when you estimate the preparation time.

House Body

To estimate the time needed to paint the house body, or walls, measure the square footage of the wall area; count the number and type of features, such

Painting Weather

The weather helps to determine how the paint and primer will bond with the surface. The ideal painting weather is mild and dry with a light breeze. Below 50° F latex paints will not work properly, and oil-based paint should be thinned with patented products that add vehicle as well as solvents. If thinner alone is used to improve the consistency of oil-based paint in cold weather, it will change the gloss.

If the weather is hot and the surface you are painting is in direct sunlight, the paint may dry so quickly that it cracks like mud on a dried-out pond. In hot weather the solvents in oil paint must be

replenished periodically to keep it thin enough to spread.

If the Surface is Wet

If the surface to be painted is even slightly damp, do not apply an oil-based product. Oil paint forms a vapor barrier as it dries. The moisture trapped on the wall behind the paint will escape, and in doing so it will lift the paint off the building. This causes blistering and bubbling.

Latex paint allows a small amount of water vapor to pass through. If the surface feels wet to the touch, it is too wet to paint; if it merely feels a little cool, which indicates the presence of a small amount of moisture, it can be painted with latex, but not with oil.

If the Paint Gets Rained On

If it rains—or if heavy dew falls on fresh paint or primer—you may or may not be in trouble.

Latex paint dries to the touch in a few hours under most conditions. However, it takes longer to cure. If the paint is still wet to the touch when it starts to rain, it will simply wash off the building. If it is just barely dry, however, it may blister or the gloss may become mottled. Because latex paint stops curing temporarily when the temperature drops below a certain point, it is best to apply it early enough in the day to give it time to dry

before the dew falls on cool nights. If a summer shower or an evening dew blisters your fresh latex, don't panic. If the paint is very fresh, the bubbles may go back down and still make a sound bond to the surface. If this hasn't happened after 24 hours, start over.

Although oil-based paint cannot be applied on a damp surface, fresh oil holds up pretty well to being rained on. If it is nearly dry, the water may only mottle the gloss. This is of no concern with primers. However, a mottled finish coat must be painted over after it is completely dry. If water gets behind the paint even more work is involved. Allow the surface to dry completely. Then prepare and paint it again.

Calculating Areas to Be Painted

1. Measure surfaces to be painted

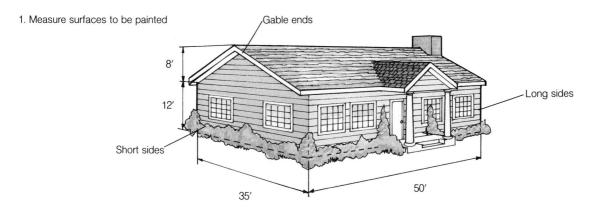

2. Calculate square footage

3. Adjust for large surfaces not to be painted

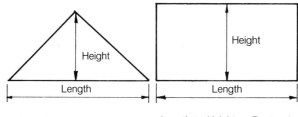

½ (Length × Height) = Triangle areas
½ (35' × 8') = 140 sq ft

Length × Height = Rectangle areas
(35' × 12') + (50' × 12') = 1,020 sq ft

Gable ends + Short sides + Long sides = Total house body
[½ (8' × 35') × 2] + [(12' × 35') × 2] + [(12' × 50') × 2] = 2,320 sq ft

as doors and windows; and then multiply these figures by the appropriate factors as given below to convert areas and numbers of objects into hours of painting work. Calculate the house body using the methods shown in the figure above. Do not subtract for openings in the wall smaller than 100 square feet. Treat the wall, doors, windows, and other features as if they formed one continuous surface.

To roll medium-textured stucco wall: 200 sq ft/hour

To roll and brush out smooth siding: 100–150 sq ft/hour

To roll and brush, or to brush, shingles: 80–125 sq ft/hour

Features

Windows are described in terms of the arrangement of the panes of glass, called lights. An ordinary sash window is thus a one-light-over-one-light window. If the upper sash contains six panes of glass, it is a six-light-over-one-light window. Descriptions of other types of windows and doors begin on page 94. The figures below are for a 3 by 5, (standard-size) window.

One-light-over-one-light window: 20 minutes

Six-light-over-one-light window: 40 minutes

Twelve-light (fixed) window: 60 minutes

Wide eaves (including the rafter tails): 50 sq ft/hour

Flush door (face and edge) and frame: 15 minutes

Paneled door (face and edge) and frame: 45 minutes

Louvered door (face and edge) and frame: 45 minutes

2 by 4 working louvered shutter (all sides): 45 minutes

Simple wrought-iron railing: 20 linear ft/hour

Lightly decorated wrought-iron railing: 10 linear ft/hour

Simple wood railing (easy to reach through): 15 linear ft/hour

Access

All of the figures given above are based on the assumption that the work is being done from the ground. Working from a ladder or scaffold takes longer.

Working from a stepladder: Add 25 to 30 percent to the estimate.

Working from a small extension ladder: Add 50 percent to the estimate.

Working from an extension ladder: Add 100 percent to the estimate.

Working from a scaffold: Add 25 to 30 percent to the estimate.

Adjustments

For overall adjustments, consider that second coats take a little less time than first coats, and that finish coats must be applied more carefully than prime coats and so take a little longer to complete.

Applying oil-based paint: Add 10 percent to basic estimate.

Applying penetrating oil sealers: Add 50 percent to basic estimate.

Applying trim color that is the same as the house body: Subtract 5 percent from basic estimate.

Applying more than one trim color: Add 10 percent to basic estimate.

Estimating Materials

Materials are estimated using the same information that was used to estimate time: the area of the house body and the number of features. The types of window and door are not important. However, the texture and the rate of absorption of the walls does have an impact on the amount of material it will take to cover them. Paint spreads farther over a sealed surface than it does over raw wood or unsealed masonry. Unless otherwise noted, the figures given below are for previously painted surfaces.

The nature of the material itself also helps to determine coverage. The figures given below are for latex house paint with a nominal coverage of 400 square feet per gallon, applied with a brush or with a brush and roller. They include an allowance for waste.

Medium-textured raw stucco wall: 150 sq ft/gallon

Medium-textured painted stucco wall: 250 sq ft/gallon

Smooth siding, new wood: 250 sq ft/gallon

Smooth siding, painted wood: 350 sq ft/gallon

Shingles, new: 200 sq ft/gallon

Factory-finished, vinyl-clad windows and doors, like those on this bungalow, do not require painting. If your house has these features, adjust the time and material estimates accordingly.

Shingles, painted: 250 sq ft/gallon

Paneled door (face and edge) and frame, raw wood: 10 doors/gallon

Paneled door (face and edge) and frame, painted: 12 doors/gallon

Flush door (face and edge) and frame, painted: 14 doors/gallon

Louvered door (face and edge) and frame, painted: 13 doors/gallon

2 by 4 working louvered shutter: 15 shutters/gallon

One-light-over-one-light window: 80 windows/gallon

Six-light-over-one-light window: 65 windows/gallon

Twelve-light window: 50 windows/gallon

Simple wood railing: 60 linear ft/gallon

If any feature is to be painted with two or more colors, figure the percentage of the feature to be painted in each color and adjust the needs accordingly.

It is always better to have slightly too much rather than too little material, particularly with specially mixed colors. It is wise to have some paint for touch-ups. You may also want to paint a fence or a mailbox to match the house in the future.

Applying six trim colors to Victorian gingerbread takes patience, but the results are spectacular.

Do It Yourself or Hire a Professional?

Painting a house is creatively rewarding and it can save you money, but it is also time-consuming, and it calls for hard physical work. While you are estimating the time and materials it will take to do the job right, ask yourself three questions.

• Do I have the time? Remember that each day requires some setup and some cleanup, so a series of short days can add up to a long job in terms of total hours.

• Do I have the stamina? Although the actual painting is not physically demanding work, other aspects of the job can be very demanding indeed. Moving large ladders, setting planks, or using a scraper for long hours all call for strength and endurance. If the access is difficult or the preparation is extensive, think twice about tackling the job yourself.

• How much will I save by doing the job myself? You must calculate your time as being worth something.

Figuring the Costs

To answer the last of these questions, you must first figure the cost of your own labor. Multiply the time estimates by minimum wage, remembering that the figures in the calculations are based on a professional painter's speed. Also remember that you may need to hire some help for certain aspects of the job. Even getting friends to pitch in will cost you lunches and cold drinks.

To the cost of labor, add estimates for the cost of materials and the cost of buying or renting tools and equipment. Compare the result to professional estimates.

If you choose to do the job yourself and ask friends or hire workers to help you, make sure that your homeowner's insurance will cover on-the-job injuries and property damage.

If you have the time, and the work is not more than you can comfortably handle, then all you have to decide is whether the satisfaction and the savings are worth the investment in time and effort.

Hiring a Professional

The first step in hiring a contractor is to find one. Or better, to find two or three. It is always best to ask several contractors to bid on a large project. Not only will their prices be different, but different contractors may place more emphasis on different aspects of the job. After reading this book, you should know what you want before you ask for bids, but the bidding process gives you an additional opportunity to refine the project.

There are several places to get names of competent contractors. The best source is satisfied customers. Ask friends and neighbors with newly painted houses if they know the name of a good painter.

Paint stores often provide the names of competent contractors who trade with them.

The store obviously has an interest in feeding potential clients to its best customers, but it also has its own reputation to protect. Stores are unlikely to refer clients to an incompetent or careless painter more than once.

Trade associations offer directories of their members. Membership requirements vary; some are very stringent, others less so. Check to see what criteria are used for membership and what criteria are used for referrals.

Specifying the Job

Before you ask for bids, understand clearly what you want the contractor to do. The better you understand the job, the better you can describe it to all of the bidders. It is important that everyone bid on the exact same job. Contractors may point out problem areas that you did not see or prefer different approaches than you had envisioned. Be sure to figure these adjustments to the various estimates. This book will help you to specify the job and to understand what the contractor is talking about.

Preparation is particularly difficult to estimate. Price variations are usually a sign that the contractors have different approaches to this part of the job. Don't be afraid to ask for a detailed commitment to a particular set of steps and standards. It is as much in the contractor's interest as it is in yours to be very clear about your expectations. Exacting preparation takes time, and time costs money. Expect to

pay for excellent preparation.

The same ideas apply in specifying materials. This book will help you to make an informed choice as to the general type of material you want for each part of the job. Each contractor will have preferred brands. Specify that appropriate materials of the highest quality be used. Difference in the price of materials is only a small percentage of the total cost of the work.

Arrange a mutually satisfactory schedule for both the work and the payments, and get it in writing, remembering that painting depends on the weather. If you need to have the work completed by a certain time, let the contractor know this when you request the bid.

Remember that the painters will be working around your home for a matter of days or weeks. Be sure to list any special requirements you want. Examples might include daily starting and quitting times (some neighborhoods have restrictions on work hours); whether the painters may play radios while they are working; whether they may bring dogs to your house; final cleanup requirements; and methods for storing and disposing of paint.

Evaluating Probable Performance

The quality of a contractor's references is very important. If you have found a contractor by means other than personal contact, ask him or her for the names of two or three satisfied customers. Then inspect those

houses, if possible, and ask those people what they think of the contractor. Be sure to get answers to the following questions.

• Is the contractor licensed? Where painting contractors are regulated by state licensing boards, you have a ready test that works in two ways. First, the contractor has had to demonstrate some competence to get a license; second, he or she must avoid gross incompetence, at the very least, to keep it. Different states hold contractors to different standards of performance and provide consumers with different means of redressing grievances.

• Does the contractor guarantee the work? Contractors should guarantee their work within reason. That is a large caveat. Paint manufacturers guarantee their product for up to 20 years. That does not mean that all of the paint on the house will look like new for 20 years. Sun, rain, freezing, and thawing all take their toll. How long the paint lasts depends on how exacting the preparation was, how well the paint was applied, the quality and type of materials, and the kind of weather the house is exposed to. You have control over the preparation and the materials when you specify the job. You can influence the application by your choice of a contractor. There is nothing you can do to make a paint job at the seashore last as long as one done inland.

• Does the contractor have insurance? The contractor should carry liability insurance appropriate to the job. From the buyer's point of view it is a plus to know that if an apprentice drops a ladder through the roof of the Rolls Royce, the contractor will have it fixed without question. Liability insurance allows small contractors to offer their customers some of the security they would normally expect only from larger companies.

• Who will do the work? Ask the contractor who will actually do the work and who will supervise. Make sure that the supervisor will be someone who understands the trade at least as well as the person who sold you the job. Some companies sell many jobs and then bid them out in turn to other contractors, keeping a percentage as their fee. This is not necessarily a bad thing, but you should ask the company point-blank if this is how they operate. If it is, demand proof that their subcontract has the exact same specifications as your original contract.

• Does the contractor have a continuing interest in your satisfaction? In the end, your goal is to find someone who knows how to do what you need done, who wants to do it, and who will do it at a price you can afford. Beyond checking the contractor's qualifications, try to find someone you can work with comfortably. The bidding process defines the job. If you communicate well at this stage, the whole job will be the better for it.

GATHERING EQUIPMENT

Painting tools help to carry the material from the bucket to the wall and to spread it smoothly and evenly precisely where you want it. Because different materials have different consistencies, specific tools are designed for use with each. Because different surfaces have different textures, painting tools are designed for use on specific surfaces.

Brushes

The painter's most useful all-around tool is the paintbrush. Even if you are rolling or spraying large areas, you will need at least one or two brushes.

Buy the best brushes available and keep them perfectly clean. The investment will save time, money, and aggravation. Poorly made brushes may save an hour's pay, but they will cost you many hours of frustration as you try in vain to make the finish coat cover in one application or to paint the window without painting the glass. Good tools in good condition are a craftsperson's joy, and you certainly deserve to share in that pleasure.

The shape, size, and composition of the brush determines the surface to use it on.

Shapes

The bristles of many brushes are trimmed square so that they all appear to be the same length. Some brushes have what is called a chiseled edge—that is, the bristles are selected for length so that the brush seems to taper to a fine edge like a cold chisel. This makes it easier to lay the paint on smoothly, without showing lap marks between one stroke and the next.

In the angle brush, or angle sash brush, the ends of the bristles would all just touch the surface if the brush were held at an angle as you would hold a pen. If the angle brush is held exactly perpendicular to the surface, only the very tip (the longest bristles) will be touching. This makes it the best brush for doing fine work, such as windows and paneled doors.

Sizes

Brushes come in a variety of widths and thicknesses. Large brushes, those which are both thick and wide, are best for carrying a lot of material to the wall and spreading it evenly over a large area. A brush 3½ to 4 inches wide will serve very well for painting most large, flat surfaces.

A 1-inch-wide, thin angle brush is the easiest to control and the easiest for a novice to use in doing detailed work. Remember, however, that so few bristles mean repeated trips to the paint bucket to get enough paint to cover anything. It is probably easier in the long run to use a larger, wider, angle brush, although learning to control it does take some time. For all but the rare fine details, you should use a brush at least 2 inches wide.

Composition

The best brushes for applying oil-based paint are made with black boar bristle, and the best bristle comes from China. Oil-based paint is stickier than latex, and the extra stiffness of boar bristle makes it easier to spread the paint smoothly and evenly. Never let a bristle brush get wet. The bristles will remember their original curly shape, and once dry the brush will look more like a rat's nest than a brush. The cheap white or cream French bristle is no substitute for China bristle.

For painting with latex and other water-based products, use brushes with bristles made from synthetic fibers, such as nylon. The best synthetic-fiber brushes do an excellent job with latex and are only slightly inferior to natural bristle for use with oil-based products.

If you are trying to save money on brushes, buy the very best synthetic-fiber 2½-inch angle brush available. Buy the thick type, not the thin sash brush. The size and shape are adequate or good for every

job, and the brush can be used with both oil-based and latex paint. Of course, if you are using the same brush for different products it must be scrupulously clean and fully dry before you make the switch. You don't want water in oil-based paint or paint thinner in latex products.

Rough-Surface Painters

Used for painting split shingles, a rough-surface painter looks like a rectangular scrub brush, with many tufts of short 1-inch to 1½-inch bristles. In addition, some versions have

Brush Types

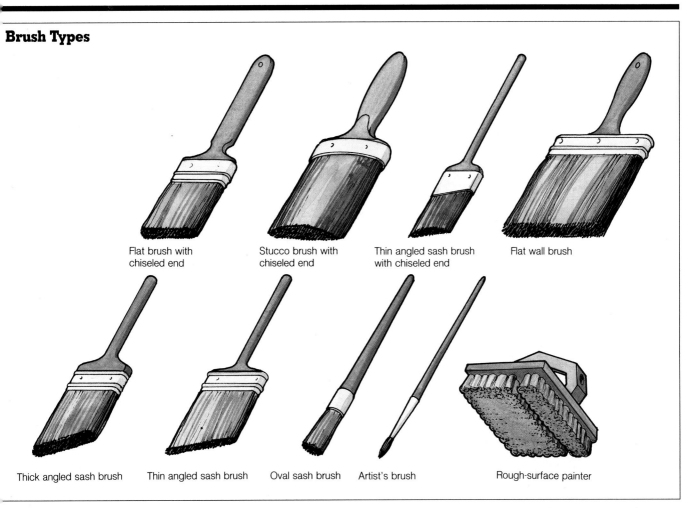

Flat brush with chiseled end

Stucco brush with chiseled end

Thin angled sash brush with chiseled end

Flat wall brush

Thick angled sash brush

Thin angled sash brush

Oval sash brush

Artist's brush

Rough-surface painter

a row of softer, more closely spaced bristles placed at an angle to the main group. The face of a split shingle has many narrow parallel grooves. The scrub brush–style bristles force the paint into the grooves and remove the excess in a single stroke. Use the row of shorter bristles to paint the bottom edge of the shingle, holding the brush at a different angle. The brush is usually adapted for mounting on a pole.

Shingle Brushes

A brush that is wide and thick at the base, with long bristles that taper to a fine edge, is very good for painting shingles. This traditional shingle brush holds plenty of material. It is flexible enough to follow the shape of the shingles and fine enough to paint the bottom edges and the narrow gaps between them.

Pads

One other type of applicator acts like a brush, though it resembles nothing else of that name. This is the painting pad. The surface of the pad looks like the smooth half of a Velcro fastener or like stiff, sparsely woven velvet. This surface corresponds to the bristles of the

brush; it holds the material and applies it to the surface being painted.

Pads are relatively inexpensive. However, they have few uses in exterior work, because they don't carry much paint, necessitating many trips to the bucket. They will smooth out paint well on flat surfaces, and they can be used for new siding or old siding in very good shape, new shingles, and very square-cut trim.

Rollers

A roller kit consists of three parts. The metal part is called the handle, frame, or cage. The part that actually picks up the paint and puts it on the wall is called the roller cover, sleeve, or nap. The third part is the tray or bucket and screen that holds the paint and allows you to remove the excess paint from the roller.

In addition, most roller handles are fitted with a female threaded connection that allows them to be screwed onto an extension pole. Poles range from simple wood handles to

Roller Equipment

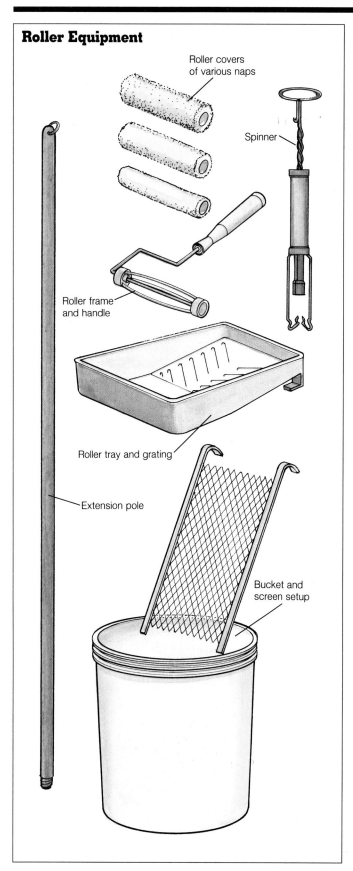

Roller covers of various naps

Spinner

Roller frame and handle

Roller tray and grating

Extension pole

Bucket and screen setup

elaborate telescoping devices of various lengths. An extension pole increases your reach and reduces the amount of bending and stooping needed to fill a roller with paint. Extension poles are available in lengths over 12 feet, but the flexibility of the pole itself will absorb much of the pressure put on it. For this reason, it may be difficult to cover heavily textured surfaces adequately in one coat using a very long extension pole. It is also difficult to see bare spots when you're viewing the work from more than 12 feet away.

Sizes

Standard paint rollers are 7 inches and 9 inches wide. Use the 7-inch width roller with a 2-gallon bucket and screen. This arrangement is handy enough to take up on a ladder. The more common 9-inch roller is used with a specially designed tray that has a deep well to hold the paint and a sloping surface for removing the excess. It is also used with a 5-gallon bucket and screen.

Covers

Roller covers come in a variety of materials, qualities, and nap lengths. Natural roller covers are made from wool—mohair for fine interior work or lamb pelts for longer-nap applications. They are expensive. Since their chief advantage is that they can be cleaned and

reused many times, the extra expense is probably not worth it for a homeowner.

Synthetic roller covers are available for use with oil-based or latex paints; most can be used with both. The chief difference between moderately priced and cheap ones is the quality of the core and the glue that holds the nap to it.

Nap length determines the surface texture that the roller creates, the amount of paint it holds, the ease with which you can apply a full coat to heavily textured surfaces, and the amount of spray you can expect. The longer the nap, the more surface texture the roller leaves, the more paint it holds, the heavier a texture it can cover, and the more you have to guard against roller spray. The shorter the nap, the less of all of these.

Generally, use the shortest nap that will do a good job. Rollers with a nap of ½ inch are fine for most applications. Rollers with shorter naps are for interior use on smooth surfaces. Use a roller with longer nap when the wall is heavily textured, with many little nooks and crannies to be filled with paint. A longer nap roller is also used to apply very heavy material, such as elastomeric sealants.

A rule of thumb is to add ¼ inch of nap for each increase in the difficulty of the surface or the material. By this method you would use a ½-inch nap to apply latex paint to a smooth, previously painted stucco wall;

a ¾-inch nap to apply the same material to a wall with some texture; and a 1-inch nap to apply latex to a heavily textured stucco wall. For applying heavy-bodied material to the same surfaces, add ¼ inch to the lengths given.

All roller covers will shed when new, but good-quality covers quickly stop shedding. Poor-quality covers continue to come apart for some time, leaving fibers in the paint. This is not a problem when applying flat wall paint to a moderately or heavily textured surface, because no one will ever notice. However, if you are using the roller to apply a gloss paint prior to brushing it out, the fibers will be obvious. To minimize this problem, rinse the roller in the appropriate cleaning agent and spin it dry before you put it into the paint (see page 104).

Sprayers

These apply paint or stain to a surface by putting it under pressure and forcing it through a small aperture, atomizing it into a cloud of tiny droplets. Conventional sprayers use compressed air. In airless sprayers, diaphragm pumps, and handheld sprayers, the paint alone is put under pressure. These last three are most commonly used in house painting. Airless sprayers and diaphragm pump sprayers are often available for rent at paint stores or equipment rental establishments.

Handheld sprayers are relatively inexpensive, but they are not usually available for rent. These sprayers have a small electric piston pump in the handheld unit. They produce less pressure and provide less control than the larger sprayers. They are useful for painting or staining latticework, railings, and other complex shapes that would be time-consuming to paint with a brush. Choose an airless or diaphragm pump sprayer if the job will take more than an hour.

Top: You can roll on paint to railings initially, but always brush it out for an even finish.
Bottom: Painting lattice with a brush alone can be time-consuming. Save time by masking and dropping carefully and applying the paint with a sprayer.

SETTING UP THE JOB

Good setup is a must for safety as well as for convenience during both the preparation and the actual painting. Access—how to get to each part of the house—must be considered early in the planning stage. Protecting plants, window glass, and other unpainted surfaces is an important part of preparation and painting.

Gaining Access

During the planning stage, figure out how to reach each part of the house. If you live in a single-level house built close to the ground, and the roofline has no gable ends or dormers, you may be able to do all the work with a good stepladder. However, most houses have at least one area that can be reached only with some other equipment.

There are several ways to estimate the height of a wall. The roughest and fastest way is to count the floors and multiply by 12 feet, the average height of one story. Remember to count the foundation or half basement and add something for the distance from the top of the upper level to the roof peaks where there are gable ends. If the wall is covered in siding or is made of brick, measure one course and count the courses to get the total height. If the house is built on a slope, the foot of the ladder will be lower than the bottom of the wall when you are painting on the downhill side.

There are several systems for gaining access to high places. The ones that are most useful for a homeowner are stepladders, extension ladders, ladder jacks and a plank, and scaffolding, sometimes called staging. Of these, stepladders and extension ladders are by far the most useful.

Whatever arrangement you use to get up in the air, remember that your life and health depend on setting the equipment properly and using it safely. A good ladder properly set is a perfectly safe platform from which to work. If it isn't properly set, or if you use it in the wrong way, you can be killed. Please use care.

The most important rule in working up in the air is always to remember where you are. All of the rules are obvious when you think about them. You will only have problems when you quit thinking about them.

Ladders

The first rule when using any type of ladder is to make sure that it is in good condition. This is relatively easy with wooden ladders, because they show their wear. Cracks or loose joints usually become visible before the ladder fails completely. When you see them, throw the ladder away. The same holds true for fiberglass ladders. With aluminum ladders damage is harder to spot. Gross defects, such as a bent rung, which should disqualify the ladder from use, are obvious, but it is impossible to see fatigued metal. The surest solution is to buy good ladders and take good care of them. Don't drop them or let them fall. Don't use them for planks. If you rent ladders from an equipment rental yard, pick the ones that show the fewest signs of abuse, such as dents or deep

Gaining access to a house with several stories takes careful planning. Consider using scaffolding on a three-story house, such as this one.

Ladder Types

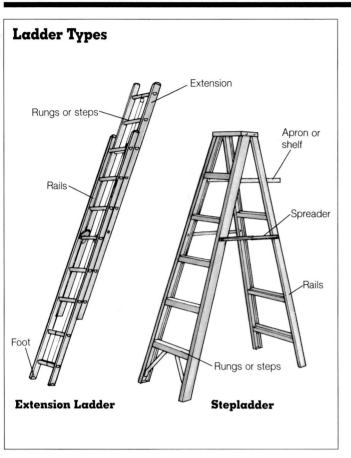

Extension

Rungs or steps

Rails

Foot

Extension Ladder

Apron or shelf

Spreader

Rails

Rungs or steps

Stepladder

scratches. Make sure that the hooks or catches, which secure one section of the ladder to another, operate smoothly. Stepladders should be inspected for the same sorts of defects and rejected or accepted on the same criteria. All moving parts should work smoothly. If you are buying a new ladder, especially a new stepladder, of course it will be a little stiff at first.

Stepladders

Stepladders come in a variety of lengths from 3 to 8 feet. Much taller stepladders are made, of course, but they're too unstable on the uneven surfaces encountered outside. The length of a stepladder is the

length of the rail that holds the rungs or steps. Stepladders are made of wood, aluminum, or in fiberglass/aluminum combinations. A stepladder should have an apron or shelf on which to set a paint bucket. The great advantage of stepladders is that they do not need to touch the wall in order to be stable. They simply need a bit of level ground. Make sure that the ladder is fully open and that the spreaders are locked into position. The ladder should not rock back and forth. Dig out under one leg or build up under another to make the stepladder stable. Do not stand on the top step as it is too easy to lose your balance there.

Tall houses can be painted from an extension ladder or a ladder jack, both of which cost less than a scaffold. However, the intricate work of painting the details of this Victorian is done most safely from a scaffold.

Extension Ladders

Available in a wide variety of lengths and load bearing classes, the nominal size of an extension ladder is the length of its side rails in feet. This is easy to see, as the rungs or steps are usually spaced one foot apart. The actual height to which the ladder will reach is slightly less than its nominal length for two reasons. First, the ladder is only used when it is at an angle, not straight up and down. The optimal angle is 75 degrees. Second, the nominal length of an extension ladder is the total length of both

sections, as if they were laid end to end. The sections must overlap by about 2 feet when they are used together, however, so a 28-foot extension ladder is really only 25 or 26 feet long when fully extended. When placed against the wall at the proper angle, the top of this ladder will hit the wall at a point about 24 feet from the ground. The foot of the ladder should be set a distance from the house equal to one fourth of the actual length of the ladder. When fully extended, the ladder in the example will be set six feet from the wall.

21

Raising a Ladder

1. Set the feet firmly against the house. Walk toward the house until the ladder is upright.

2. When carrying a ladder upright, keep it vertical.

Leveling legs

Blocks

3. Level the legs with blocks or special leveling legs, which are part of the ladder.

Ladders are classified according to their load bearing capacity. Those from one manufacturer, for example, are rated class 1 = 200 pound; class 2 = 225 pound; class 3 = 300 pound. The higher numbered classes are more heavily built and so are rated as being able to hold greater weight safely. The federal government requires ladder manufacturers to test their products to a safety factor of three times the rated weight. This means that the class 1 ladder from this manufacturer can hold 200 pounds with a safety factor of three or a static weight of 600 pounds (3 × 200). The higher the weight rating, the stiffer the ladder will be. This can be a very comforting thing, especially on a tall ladder. Unfortunately, the more stoutly built the ladder is, the heavier it is to carry. The actual weight of a 20 foot aluminum extension ladder from this same manufacturer is: class 1 = 24 pound; class 2 = 33 pound; class 3 = 43 pound. For a 28-foot ladder, the figures would be: class 1 = 40 pound; class 2 = 45 pound; class 3 = 57 pound. Fifty-seven pounds may not sound like much to you, but when it is distributed along a twenty-five foot ladder and has all that leverage, it can be very hard work to make it go where you want it to.

Using Ladders

Even if you are young and strong, it is best to substitute brains for brawn when moving ladders. When moving the ladder any distance, it is best to retract it to its shortest length.

If there is a line and pulley for raising the second section, make sure that the line is secured to one of the rungs with all the excess line taken up so it doesn't drag on the ground and catch something or trip you. Carry the ladder at the level of your hips like a piece of luggage. Carrying things higher than this puts unnecessary strain on the lower back. Use both hands to make it easier to guide around objects ahead of and behind you!

When you get the ladder to the place where you want to use it, set it up.

Scaffolding

When the area to be worked on is high and the amount of work to be done is great, scaffolding is required. Scaffolding can be rented in metropolitan areas from contractors who will install and remove the scaffolding for you. Rental is generally by the month or week. If there is enough work to justify scaffolding the house, seriously consider hiring out not only the scaffolding but the work as well.

Ladder Jacks

For the vast majority of houses, ladder jacks and planks on a pair of extension ladders form a version of scaffolding that is easily set up and moved by two people. This will serve very well for working on those areas where there is a lot of scraping and grinding to do or where setting a single ladder in the right spot would be difficult.

Ladder jacks are like adjustable shelf brackets used to hold a plank. The ladder jacks slip over the rungs of the ladder.

Correct Ladder Angles

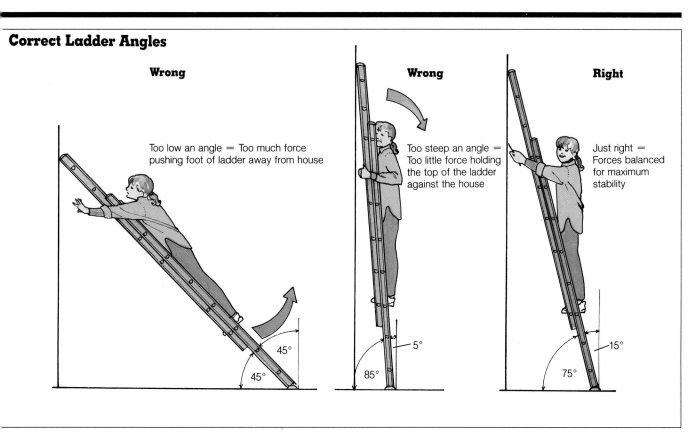

Wrong

Too low an angle = Too much force pushing foot of ladder away from house

45°

45°

Wrong

Too steep an angle = Too little force holding the top of the ladder against the house

5°

85°

Right

Just right = Forces balanced for maximum stability

15°

75°

The angle between the bracket and the part that slips over the rungs is adjustable so it can be used in various positions and still hold the plank level. Setting a plank and ladder jacks is a two person operation.

Using Scaffolding

Working from a plank takes a bit of care and practice. The plank has a bit of spring to it, so it sways slightly when you move on it. When two people are working on the plank they must keep each other posted and make no sudden unannounced movements. Remembering where you are is more important when working from a plank than anywhere else. They are only one foot wide, so there is absolutely no room for daydreaming.

Planks are either a single solid wood board or aluminum formed like the cross section of an airplane wing (sometimes covered with a plywood surface). Of the two, the aluminum is far preferable. Except for overcoming very rare access problems, planking is too much trouble to use if the plank is less than 16 feet long. Shorter lengths require too many moves of the setup. Aluminum planks of 16 to 24 feet are heavy, but manageable. Wooden planks of 16 feet or more are very heavy, very awkward, and not as stiff as aluminum planks of the same length. Planks can be rented from the same places that rent ladders. The same cautions that apply to choosing aluminum ladders also apply to aluminum planks.

Setting Up a Ladder Jack

Extension ladder

Painter

Extension ladder

Aluminum plank

Bracket

Bracket

Dropping and Masking

Protecting the things you don't want to paint is an important part of the job. Use drop cloths to protect walkways, patios, decks, and plants. Protect things that can't be covered with a cloth or a sheet of plastic by masking them with paper or plastic secured with tape.

How much you need to cover depends on how big a mess you are likely to make. When painting a window with a brush, use a small drop cloth directly beneath the work area. When rolling on material, cover an area 6 to 10 feet from the wall, depending on how much roller spray you expect. When using a sprayer, cover a wider area; the wind will carry overspray for a surprisingly far distance.

Drops

Standard painter's drop cloths are made of canvas. For most houses two or three 9 by 12 cloths will satisfy all dropping requirements. Canvas drops are thick enough to absorb and stop all but the worst paint spills, heavy enough to stay put, and rugged enough to stand up to being walked on without tearing. Plastic sheeting is inexpensive, but it makes for a slippery work surface and it tears easily.

Protecting Plants

Use old bed sheets to protect plants. They are too thin to stop more than a light spray of paint, but they stop dust and paint chips very well, and their lightness keeps them from crushing the plants. Do not use plastic to cover plants for more than a few minutes. The sunlight hitting the plastic will heat up the air inside and steam them. Plants need to breathe.

Trim plants far enough back from the house to keep them from touching the fresh paint. For easier access, pull back shrubs with a rope secured to a stake driven into the ground. Put a drop cloth or sheet around the shrub and tie back the corners like a sail to keep all of the tiny branches off the wall. A pattern of stakes driven into the ground can also hold drop cloths above tender plantings, but remember that you will need to stand somewhere. A few drops of paint will do less damage than your foot. It may be better to leave the plants uncovered, so that you can be sure where you are stepping.

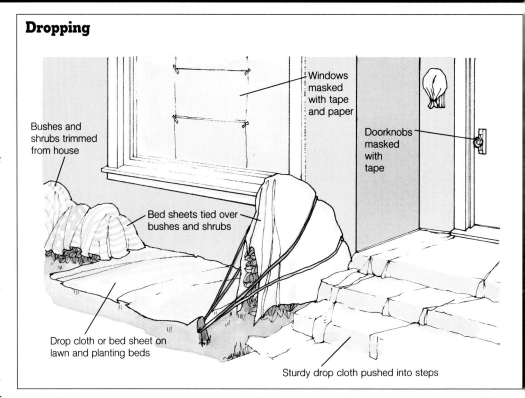

Dropping

Windows masked with tape and paper

Bushes and shrubs trimmed from house

Doorknobs masked with tape

Bed sheets tied over bushes and shrubs

Drop cloth or bed sheet on lawn and planting beds

Sturdy drop cloth pushed into steps

Masking

Masking machine

Tape all doorknobs to protect them when the door is painted and from painter's hands

When using chemicals, such as chlorine bleach solution for killing mildew or acids for etching metal or concrete, protect nearby plants by soaking them throughly with water first. This will prevent the plants from absorbing any chemicals that might splash onto them. If you are using strong caustics, such as paint strippers, cover the plants with drops as well. After you have finished using the chemicals, rinse nearby plants with water.

Using Drops

When you lay out the drop cloths, try to cover one entire side of the house. Constantly shifting drop cloths can leave a trail of paint chips, which must then be cleaned up.

Be careful when you walk over drop cloths. The edges can catch your foot or the foot of the ladder you are carrying. They can also conceal unevenness in the ground. Press the drop cloth smoothly and tightly against steps, so that there is no excess material to trip over.

From time to time check the edge of the drop cloth that is nearest the wall, especially when rolling on a coat of paint. Drop cloths have a tendency to pull away from the wall when you walk on them.

Masking

You need to mask most extensively to protect window glass, prefinished gutters, and so forth when spraying. When brushing or rolling, you have more control over where the paint goes, so you can mask less. However, rollers create a small amount of spray so mask a wider area.

Light fixtures or other hardware can be masked rather than removed. If you have a natural-wood railing that butts into the body of the house, you might want to mask the first few inches of it in case the drop cloth pulls back slightly when you are rolling or brushing near it. Except when the house is to be sprayed, it is easier to keep the windows clean than it is to mask them. Prefinished gutters are also easy to keep clean by being careful, but prefinished downspouts may be worth masking if you plan to roll above them or next to them. This is especially true where the downspouts are too high for you to clean off from a stepladder.

Use tape and paper or plastic to mask. If something is to be masked to make a clean edge, it is easiest to put down the tape first. Make sure not to cover any part of the surface to be painted. It is very discouraging to see a bit of the old color when the masking tape is pulled off. When you have put down the tape, cover the rest of the surface to be protected with paper or plastic sheeting secured with more tape. Make sure that the surface is completely protected, and that there is no loose masking material to get into the fresh paint.

The glue used in standard masking tape has an unhappy tendency to become more attached to the surface than it was to the tape. The longer it stays in place, the more pronounced this attachment becomes, until you would swear it had bonded chemically to the surface. Standard painter's masking tape is only slightly better. However, some newer drafting-style masking tapes will stay up for a week or more and pull off cleanly from sound surfaces, leaving no residue. They are quite a bit more expensive than the standard tape and worth every penny.

Masking tape does not adhere well to brick and masonry. It helps to brush off loose dirt and dust before you apply it. Better yet, use duct tape for masking masonry. It always leaves a little glue behind, and it can easily pull off paint from the surface, but it's still the best product for masking rough surfaces.

Masking machines are available that automatically attach tape to one edge of a strip of masking paper as it is pulled from a roll. These machines are expensive (you can buy three or four good brushes for the price of a masker), but they may be worth the price if you have many windows and intend to spray the house.

Unusual windows, such as these round ones, require good painting technique. Although this work is tedious, it will eliminate hours of window scraping later.

# CHOOSING COLORS

House painting serves a dual purpose: It protects the house structure and it serves as a vehicle for creative expression. This chapter explains how to use color to express your individual taste. It contains specific guidelines to the color-selecting process, including the use of the color wheel. It includes photographs of beautifully color-coordinated houses to provide you with inspiration. The proper use of color shows the house to its best advantage; it accentuates architectural features and it enhances the natural beauty of the landscaping. Knowing how colors work together allows you to create harmonious effects.

This white house, with its accents of yellow and red, is a delightful example of the judicious use of a primary color. Use the color wheel to learn how to combine colors effectively.

Color has always had a profound influence on the human psyche. Basic knowledge of color theory and keen personal observation are required to understand this influence. They will provide the guidelines you will need in order to express your individual taste.

The Color Spectrum

In 1666 Sir Isaac Newton identified the solar color spectrum when he observed that sunlight passing through a prism forms a rainbow of colors consisting of red, orange, yellow, green, blue, indigo, and violet. The color of light is determined by its wavelength. Different wavelengths produce different colors. Nothing—including paint pigments—has color in and of itself, but the eye responds to particular wavelengths of light reflected back from objects to form an impression of their color. The spectrum—simplified to six colors by substituting purple for indigo and violet—contains the three primary and three secondary colors used to form the color wheel.

The Color Wheel

This is an extremely useful tool. It displays an inventory of basic colors, identifies the transition from color to color through the visible spectrum, and shows how colors are related to one another.

The color wheel contains, first, the primary colors—red, yellow, and blue. They are called primary colors because they cannot be produced by mixing together any other colors. The secondary colors—orange, green, and purple—are produced by mixing pairs of primary colors. Red and yellow produces orange; yellow and blue produces green; and red and blue produces purple. Completing the color wheel are the intermediate colors, mixtures of primary and secondary colors. These 12 full-strength colors are known as pure hues, meaning that no neutral colors—white, black, or gray—have been added to them.

Neutral Colors

Black, white, and gray are not colors in the defined sense, yet they play a very important role in creating a balanced and varied color scheme. Use them for contrast, to break up a color scheme, or as an accent.

There are many shades of each neutral color. There are, for example, red-black, blue-black, and green-black. All of these appear as dark as pure black (often called lamp black), but they have more depth and richness.

True pure white is seldom used in house painting. Usually, some element of color is added, ranging from the barely perceptible to a full off-white tint of color. To give variety and subtlety to your color scheme, choose a white that contains a small amount of color analogous to, or contrasting with, the basic colors.

The range of grays is also very wide. Choose a gray that is analogous to your basic colors, such as a blue-gray used with other blues or a brown-gray used with other browns.

Neutral colors are also mixed with pure hues to create tints, shades, and tones.

Tints, Shades, and Tones

Because they are so intense, the colors of the color wheel are seldom used in their pure-hue form except as accents. More often, variations of these colors,

Tints, tones, and shades of blue—along with white accents—form an analogous color scheme. An analogous scheme creates a soothing and subtle effect, a good choice for a grand entrance.

created by adding white, black, or gray, are used. When white is added to a color, a tint of that color is created, which is lighter in value than the pure hue. When black is added to a color, a shade of that color is created, which is darker in value than the pure hue. When gray—both black and white—is added to a color, a tone of that color is created, which is muted compared to the pure hue.

Color Harmony

There are two basic methods of selecting colors for a harmonious color scheme. Analogous harmony combines colors that are adjacent to or near each other on the color wheel, such as blue and blue-green or yellow and orange-yellow. Complementary, or contrast, harmony combines colors that are across from each other on the color wheel, such as blue and orange or yellow and purple. A harmony of mutual complements is a hybrid method combining analogous and complementary colors, such as yellow, yellow-green, green, and red-purple.

Whichever method you use, remember that paint colors will not be the pure hues of the color wheel but relative values of those colors—that is, tints, shades, and tones. It is important to consider the relationship of lightness to darkness within your color selections as well as the relationships among the colors themselves.

The section on choosing a color scheme begins on page 32. The examples given on the following pages will help you to understand the concept of color harmony.

The Color Wheel

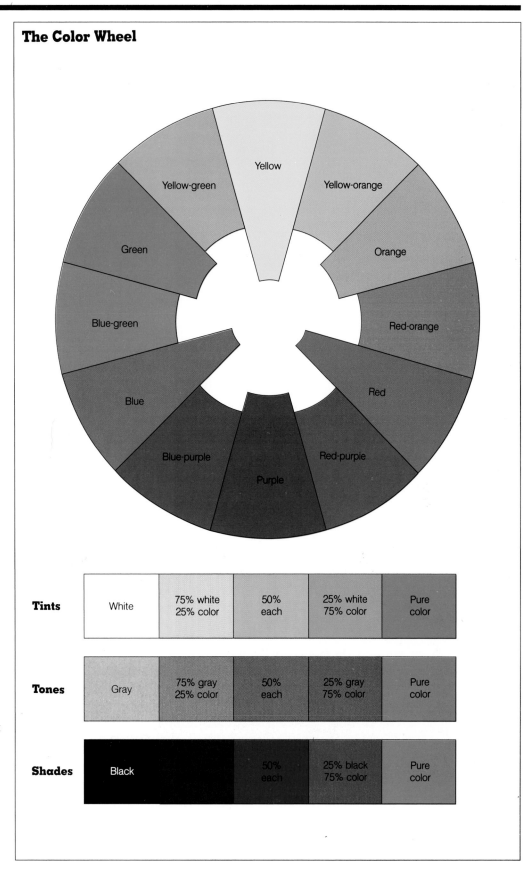

Tints	White	75% white 25% color	50% each	25% white 75% color	Pure color

Tones	Gray	75% gray 25% color	50% each	25% gray 75% color	Pure color

Shades	Black		50% each	25% black 75% color	Pure color

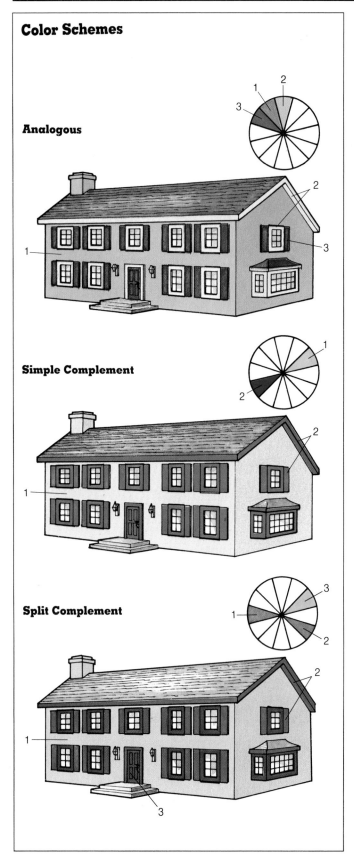

Color Schemes

Analogous

Simple Complement

Split Complement

Analogous Colors

Colors that are adjacent to or near each other on the color wheel are analogous. Tints, shades, and tones of analogous colors offer a limitless supply of options.

As a rule, up to five adjacent colors can form an analogous scheme. (More than five positions infringe on the field belonging to the next primary color.) Yellow, yellow-orange, orange, red-orange, and red are all analogous to one another. A scheme based on these colors might begin with house siding left natural brown (brown is a shade of orange). Choose a tone of yellow-orange (off-white beige) for the body of the house, another shade of orange (brown) for the fascias and eaves, a tint of yellow-orange (peach) for the windows, and an almost pure hue of orange as an accent color for the front door.

An example of an analogous color scheme based around green landscaping and incorporating pure white is a tint of blue (an off-white lilac) for the house body, a pure white for the fascias and eaves, and a tone of blue-green for the windows and doors.

An analogous color scheme can also be formed by using variations of one color. If the finish roof is blue, choose an off-white tint of blue for the house body, a tone of blue-gray for the windows, a deep shade of blue for the fascias and eaves, and black in the wrought-iron railings.

A walk through any neighborhood will reveal many examples of analogous color

schemes. Although they lack the boldness of strong contrast, analogous color combinations do create a subtle, soft effect.

Complementary Colors

Colors that are directly across from each other on the color wheel are complementary. For example, green is the complement of red, and blue-green is the complement of red-orange. Like other colors, complementary colors are seldom used in their pure hues. Choose relative values when selecting a house color scheme.

An example of a complementary color scheme based on a terra-cotta roof would be a light tone of red-orange for the body, a dark shade of red-orange for the fascias and eaves, and the complementary shade of blue-green for the windows and doors. Another example of a complementary color scheme would be a light, almost off-white, tone of peach (yellow-orange) for the body with a slightly grayed tone of blue-purple on the trim. Both of these examples use strong color contrast to create a feeling of harmony.

Simple two-color complementary color schemes don't always provide enough variety. If this is a problem, consider multiple-color split complements, double complements, and color triads.

Split Complements

One way of increasing the color palette while staying within the confines of a complementary harmony is to use the split complement. The split complement divides the complement of one color into its two adjacent colors. For example, red-orange is the complement of blue-green. The split complement of blue-green would be orange and red. A split-complement color scheme is a light muted blue-green for the house body; a dark shade of orange for the windows, fascias, and eaves; and a more or less pure hue of red for the windowsills, doors, and railings.

The benefits of increasing the complementary palette become more evident when unpainted features are included. An example based on a red brick house would be to choose a shade of blue for the fascias and eaves and a tint of green for the windows and doors.

Double Complements

Here is another way to increase the variety of a color palette. A double complement is formed by splitting two complementary colors to their adjacent colors. Yellow is the complement of purple; yellow-orange and yellow-green are the double complements of red-purple and blue-purple.

One example using this color scheme incorporates a shade of red in the bricks of the body of the house; a grayed tone of blue on the windows, doors, and trim; brown on the walkways and decks; and a light tone tan on the fascias and eaves. This scheme will balance nicely with green in the shrubs, plants, and lawn, creating a varied but balanced harmony of colors.

Color Triads

The triad method gives you a wide choice of interesting color combinations. Place an equilateral triangle over the color wheel to divide it into three equal parts. The colors on the points of the triangle form a triad. An example is orange, green, and purple. A color scheme based on this triad would consist of light orange cedar shingles on the body of the house; a light tone of green for the windows and doors; and a very dark shade of purple for the fascias, eaves, and railings. The harmonies produced with triads are soft, delicate, and intricate.

Mutual Complements

A mutual complement combines the harmony of analogy with the harmony of contrast. It does this by combining the colors of an analogous family with a single contrasting color. The contrasting color should be a complement of the median value of the analogous family. For instance, if the analogous colors are red-orange, orange, and yellow-orange, the median color is orange and the contrasting color is blue.

An example of this color scheme would be yellow-orange (creamy beige) for the house body, brown for the fascias and window sashes, and a tone of red-orange (red clay) for the window moldings and the eaves. To this very soft and subtle harmony add a blue front door or railings, to create a bold, interesting contrast.

If an analogous color scheme appeals to you, it is worthwhile to see whether the complement of the analogous colors would add variety.

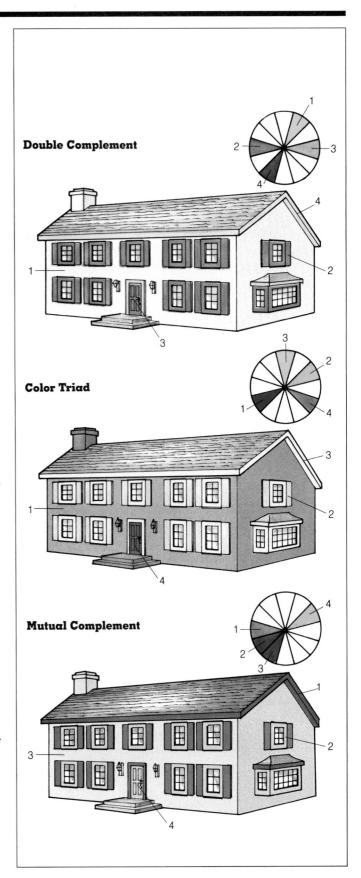

Double Complement

Color Triad

Mutual Complement

DESIGNING A COLOR SCHEME

There are no right or wrong colors to paint a house. Choosing a color scheme is a matter of finding colors you like, coordinating them with the fixed colors and surfaces of the house, and deciding what to emphasize. It's not a difficult task; just test and eliminate alternatives until the final colors come together.

Note: If you live in an area where there are codes, covenants, and restrictions on exterior colors, be sure to obtain these guidelines before you choose a color scheme.

Gather Ideas

The first task in choosing a color scheme is to become aware of color. The object is not so much to be able to name the colors as it is to really see them.

Gather the information you need. Then let your mind do the work. Give yourself plenty of time to mull over color options. Working on the puzzle for 5 minutes in the morning and 10 minutes at night for 2 weeks is much more productive than spending 3 hours on it all at once.

There are many sources of color ideas. Don't try to keep them all in your mind's eye. Begin a scrapbook or file folder in which to keep magazine pictures of houses you like, swatches of fabric, addresses of nicely painted houses in the neighborhood, and so forth. This is a handy way to compare different combinations.

Photographs

Pictures in books and magazines can be a great source of color ideas. The photographs in this book are an obvious place to start, but the pictures don't have to be of houses to be a source of color inspiration.

Whatever the source and whatever the subject, a few cautions apply when you look at photographs. First, try to see what it is that makes the picture appealing. It may not be the color per se, but rather the general ambience. This leads to the second caution: Be sure you know what color you are looking at. The soft focus and special lighting effects so popular in advertising photographs can make it difficult to identify exact colors. It's easier if you block out the rest of the picture with white paper. You may find too that what looks like one color is actually dozens of colors all mixed together. The effect of these mottled colors is very different from the effect of one solid color.

Be aware of scale when you look at colors in photographs. A color that looks great in a 1-inch-square section of a picture may well be overpowering on the side of a house. Rather than matching colors exactly, try mixing a tint or a tone of the color to achieve the same effect on a larger scale.

Fabrics

Fabric stores are another great source of inspiration. Printed fabrics combine colors imaginatively. You may be able to use a swatch of a printed fabric for all the colors on the house. Many prints are created by famous designers whose sense of color has been honed by years of education and practice.

Look around your house for fabrics. Clothes, upholstery materials, window treatments, carpets, and bedding all reflect your taste in color. They can be a good place to start building awareness of color and generating ideas. If the interior of the house has a dominant color scheme, consider using the same colors for the exterior.

Some of the same cautions apply to fabrics as to photographs. Be sure you are looking at a single color, and beware of picking colors that are too intense for a large area.

Other Houses

Walk through the neighborhood to see how other people have solved the puzzle you are working on. A walk helps in several ways. First, it shows you exactly how a certain color looks on a house—something that you cannot learn from photographs and fabrics. Second, it shows how other people have used color to deal with line and form. Third, it will

Opposite: You can get color ideas from different parts of the house. The colors of this wonderful Bernard Maybeck–designed cottage came from those of the stained glass window above the garage.
Above: Bring out the interesting details of even the simplest house with a triad color scheme.

Manufacturers' Samples

Paint manufacturers produce paper color samples, called swatches, covering their entire line. They also have brochures showing houses painted with their products and charts showing gloss levels, stain colors, and porch and deck paints. These are a great way to get color ideas, especially since the colors can be readily tested. Information about finding and using samples begins on page 48.

Art Supply Stores

For anyone interested in color, spending time in an art store is like spending time in a candy store when you were a kid. Every color of the rainbow can be found there in one medium or another: oils, pastels, crayons, inks, colored pens and pencils, and plastic film.

Consider picking up some colored pencils in colors you especially like and using them to color in a black-and-white photocopy of a picture of your house. If you are feeling ambitious and you have the talent, make outline drawings of various faces of the house, photocopy these, and color them in various schemes.

If you do this, here are two points to remember. First, beware of the difference in scale between a drawing and a building. Colors may have to be toned down to look good at full scale. Second, not every color is easy to reproduce in house paint. Most house paints have at least some white pigment in them, and this limits the range of colors. Pure, or nearly pure, hues can be made,

probably provide examples of how to do it wrong. This is almost more valuable than examples of how to do it right. Finally, it reminds you of the context within which your house will be seen. This is not to suggest that you should paint your house just like the others. Far from it; but it can be a big help when dealing with overall design issues to see your house as a stranger might see it.

Visit local historic houses, especially if your house is in the same architectural style. If they have been restored, they will be painted in the colors of the period. Tour model homes to see the popular colors that brand-new houses are being painted.

Top: Consider seasonal surroundings when choosing house colors. A light yellow and white house forms a backdrop for a spring prairie garden.
Bottom: Warm tones of brown and highlights of yellow on this Victorian marry well with fall colors.

but the paint store supplier may need to order special bases to do it (see page 48).

Determine Fixed Colors

With such a wealth of color and such seemingly infinite possibilities, you need some way to limit the choices to a manageable number. Taste is the first consideration. Some people just don't like blue, for example, or would never dream of painting their house orange. However, there is another way to limit the choices, and that is to look at the fixed colors of the house.

Walk around the house noting all the features that cannot or will not be painted. Note both the color and the texture of these features. Keep in mind that the colors you choose for the body and trim of the house will be seen next to these fixed colors. Don't feel imprisoned by these colors. It is more important that your color scheme be harmonious in itself. Nevertheless, because of the way people perceive color, these nearby colors will alter the overall effect of your scheme. For example, a blue-green will look blue next to a green wall and green next to a blue one. See pages 30 and 31 for a distilled discussion of the ways in which colors react with one another. Be sure to use this information when you choose your color scheme.

The Roof

Many roofing materials are fairly neutral. The more neutral they are, the less impact they will have on the color scheme.

Top: Remember the fixed colors of the house when choosing paint. On this ranch house, the gray roof was the fixed color from which the scheme was derived. The pink accents on the shutters reflect a color in the masonry. Bottom: A green house hides in its lush garden, allowing the blooming shrubs to stand out.

If the roof is brightly colored and high pitched, so that it makes up a large part of the overall impression of the house, then it must be given real weight in the scheme. If you have a new shake roof, be aware that it will weather to gray. A new copper roof will weather to green. A new tin roof should be painted whatever color you want it to be.

Unpainted Wood

Wood shakes and siding can be left natural, stained, or painted. If wood is to be left natural, its natural color forms part of the color scheme. Stains are available in a number of colors, which may change the color of the wood. If you wish to paint wood shakes or siding, the texture will affect the color of the paint.

Don't forget other items of unpainted wood. Note the colors of fences and decks, especially those right next to the house. These can be treated as fixed colors, or the items can be stained or painted to form part of the new color scheme.

Masonry

Brick and stonework—on the house, pathways, patios, and garden walls—have a predominant color that must be taken into account when choosing colors for the rest of the house. Unpainted concrete is so neutral that it needn't be high on the list of color priorities. However, some types of brick and all types of natural stone actually have multiple colors. A close look will reveal these and may even be a source of inspiration in choosing other colors for the house. Flagstone and outcrops of living rock are treated like other forms of masonry. The predominant color is the most important one to consider, but other colors may be brought out by choosing paint colors that complement them. Of course, masonry can also be painted.

Top: Investigate color combinations wherever you find them. Hot pink, lilac, and purple are unusual choices for a house, but they match perfectly the colors of the fuschia blooming in front of this Victorian town house. Bottom: Plain black and white trim allows the spectacular stonework of this house to dominate.

Plants

The color of the trees and grass around a house influences the onlooker's perception of its color scheme. The same is true of all ornamental plantings, flower beds, and so on. This can be a tricky issue, since the colors of plants change through the seasons in most parts of North America. The simplest approach is to consider the background colors to be the greens of the growing season. The muted browns and grays of the temperate fall and winter are more neutral colors, and therefore exert less influence on the color scheme.

If you have blooming shrubs or flower beds near the house, consider choosing colors for the house that will set off the colors of the blooms.

Nearby Buildings

Other buildings on your property are, of course, under your control. Unfortunately, neighboring houses are not. If the nearby structures are public buildings, there is a better than even chance that the colors will not change much over time, so they can be treated as fixed. Neighboring houses are a different story. They could change colors at any time. The best thing to do is to ignore them and make sure that your design suits your taste and the more immediate surroundings of the house.

Emphasize the Line of the House

Color can make a house look taller or wider, make it stand out from or blend into its surroundings. Paint will not change the actual shape of the house, but it can change the way it seems to be shaped. Paint will not change the texture of its surface, but color can make that texture more or less apparent. A coat of paint will change the size of the house only by a few thousandths of an inch, but if you paint it all white, for example, it will appear larger than it would if you painted it all dark brown.

Take a walk around the house; try to see it as just another object of a certain size, shape, and texture. In addition to the overall shape of the building, look at the secondary lines and shapes. Note the roofline; whether the eaves are open or boxed; the arrangement of the windows, as well as the intricacy of the frames and the placement of the sashes; the number and the placement of the doors and their frames. Note the strong horizontal lines of the siding, the patterns of the brick or shingles, the strong vertical lines of the downspouts and the horizontal line of the gutters.

Color can be used to emphasize some of these shapes and to make others fade into the background. In the simplest case, if the whole house is painted white, none of these elements will be given precedence over any other. The architectural details and the shape of the building will speak for themselves, without additions or amendments. At the opposite end of the scale, if the whole house is painted dark brown, the front door-frame only is painted white, and the front door itself is painted red, the doorway will draw the eyes of every onlooker. The response will be so strong, in fact, that most people will notice very little about the rest of the house except its general outline.

Define the House Outline

When deciding what colors should go where, try to see the whole house as a unified composition. It may help to imagine

Emphasize the width of a house by painting the horizontal features in contrast to the main body. The brown stripe painted midway up across this Georgian Revival house draws the eye from side to side.

Top: Classic architectural styles lend themselves to classic color combinations. A Tudor house is traditionally painted with an off-white body and dark brown trim.
Bottom: Mediterranean houses work well painted in earth tones, which mimic their original adobe construction.

the house as painted all in white. You would like the composition to be balanced and yet have some tension or interest. Think about which lines and forms you would like to emphasize and which you would like to blend into the background. Imagine what the house would look like if only the horizontal trim were painted in a color. Only the vertical trim? In this way, you take the complexity of color out of the equation temporarily in order to concentrate on line and form.

Make Colors Work for the House

Your house embodies the taste of the architect and the builder, and of their time and place. This sets certain limits for your color scheme in terms of line and form. If the architecture of the house is at one extreme, your color choices cannot take it all the way to the other. However, you can make a gesture toward symmetry or asymmetry, toward balance or tension. The greater the differences between the various colors in the color scheme, the greater the tension will be. If the more intense colors are used sparingly, the effect can be well balanced and yet add interest to the overall design.

There are guidelines to make the color scheme work for the house architecture.

• To make the house look larger, paint it a light color.

• To emphasize the trim, plan a high contrast between the house body color and the trim color. Paint the house body dark and the trim light for greatest impact.

• To de-emphasize multiple textures, paint them all the same color.

• To make a house look taller, emphasize the vertical trim lines, including columns and railings, by painting them in a color that contrasts with the house body.

• To make a house look wider, emphasize the horizontal lines, including the fascia, the roofline trim, and the trim of horizontal windows, by painting them in a color that contrasts with the house body.

• To make the house blend into its surroundings, avoid colors that contrast with those surroundings.

• Paint roof vents to blend with the roof color or to match other metal elements; paint gutters the same color as the eaves and fascias; paint downspouts the same color as the house body.

Stop to Consider

Wherever you get your ideas for colors, you must translate those ideas into actual house paint, stain, or other finish material and decide what sections of the house will be painted in each color. Before you choose a final color scheme, read about detailing and special effects (see page 40) and using wood stains and other materials (see page 44). It is also very important to shop for paint samples and test them on the house (see page 48) before you make your final decision.

Color Matching

Many paint stores will match colors for you, either by eye or with the aid of computerized color-matching scanners. Nearly any item can be matched: A color scheme can be based on your true love's eyes, existing paint, a piece of fabric, or just about anything else. A sample of at least 1 square inch is necessary in order to get a true color reading from a computer scanner. Larger samples are needed for matching by eye.

You don't have to be a professional to match paint formulas. If you prefer to try your hand at it, color matching can be rewarding.

Matchmaking

Start with a sample about 4 inches square. It can be on almost any surface. When matching colors in photographs, bear in mind that the lighting in the picture can mottle or soften the intensity of the color. You may have to mix a lighter version to achieve the same effect. Fabric or rug samples may be not one solid color but a woven blend of different colored threads. To reduce these samples to one color, look at them from a distance or squint. Of course, this is impossible for a computerized scanner to do, so samples of this type can be matched only by eye.

When matching an old exterior painted surface, beware of color variations caused by fading. This is particularly important if you intend to repaint only a portion of the building using the old color. Sunlight and other weather factors change the color over time,

bleaching and fading it. Darker colors are particularly susceptible, since they absorb more energy from the sunlight. One way to see this fading effect is to remove a piece of trim or a strip of peeling paint from the house and hold it next to other parts. The difference in color, if there is one, will become apparent.

Once you have defined the color to be matched, find the paint swatch cards that most closely resemble it. Ask the paint store to make up a sample quart of each color in latex, since latex dries fast and is easy to clean up.

Have on hand some white card stock or white paper for recording the color changes. Buy some white paint of the same type as the samples for making tints of each color, and buy a set of pigments.

Universal tinting colors are the best pigments to use because they can be mixed in both latex and oil-based paints. A complete set of pigments will consist of 12 colors: lamp black, burnt umber, raw umber, burnt sienna, raw sienna, orange, violet, red, thalo green, thalo blue, light yellow, and medium yellow. Of course, you need purchase only those pigments appropriate to your color match.

Apply the color samples to the house as described on page 48. The object is to apply the sample colors, adjust them by adding white paint or pigments, test the adjusted colors, and continue in this fashion until you get the colors you want.

Take a good look at the samples once they are dry. They may match perfectly, or one of the colors may be preferable to your original choice. Sometimes the color to be matched will fall between two of the sample quarts. In that case, try mixing the samples together.

Begin with a half-and-half mixture of the two colors. Brush a sample of this mixture onto the wall in a new area. Brush a bit of the same mixture onto a piece of paper to make a portable record. Label the paper to show what colors were mixed in what proportions to arrive at this color. Let this mixture dry before you decide whether the color is right or not.

If the color is basically right, but it seems too dark, lighten it by adding a *small* amount of white paint. (Just a little at a time—it's impossible to go backward in this process.)

If the color is not right, alter it by adding the appropriate pigments. A tiny amount of pigment can change the color of the paint dramatically. It will take longer to mix the drop or two of pigment in thoroughly with the sample than it did to mix in the white paint, so stir the mixture well before you put your brush in it. In every case, keep track of the mixtures by making swatches of likely candidates, as described above.

When you find the color you want, there are two ways to get the right amount of paint in this color. You can have the store mix paint from your sample or you can mix it yourself.

Mixing It Up

If the paint store is to mix the color, provide them with your sample. The store has a machine that will deliver pigment in increments of $\frac{1}{32}$ ounce, called points of colorant. This gives them greater precision in mixing colors than you can achieve by hand. This precision means that a formula can be written down and more paint of the same formula can be made. Ask the store to make a single quart of the color in the type of paint that you will actually be using. Test this first quart to see that the color has remained true by painting some of it onto the card stock sample. If it is not correct, ask the paint store to adjust it. When the formula is correct, write it down, being sure to note the base and type of paint used.

To mix colors yourself, begin with white paint or some other appropriate base (see page 48). Follow the exact procedure used for mixing a sample color. Be sure to make up enough paint to meet your needs, including any second or third coats and touch-ups. As a matter of practice, you would usually mix the colors yourself only if you needed a small quantity, as for an accent color.

Whether the paint store mixes it for you or whether you do it yourself, mix the contents of every container with those of every other container before you use any paint. This is called boxing the material; it is done to ensure uniformity of color.

DETAILING AND ADDING SPECIAL EFFECTS

Houses can be painted one color, multiple colors, or with a variety of special effects. It takes a bit more time to paint the windows, doors, and trim a different color than the house body, and special effects are more labor-intensive than standard painting, but the rewards can be very great.

Detailing

In its broadest sense, detailing simply means painting the trim a different color than the body of the house. Some houses, particularly the Victorians and other nineteenth-century styles, offer great opportunities for detailing because they have a wealth of features that can be highlighted with paint.

Painting one type of ornament in a given color wherever it appears on the house adds visual interest and unifies the overall design.

Using several colors to pick out the details of one centrally placed decoration, such as a complex carving, can be very effective too, particularly if the rest of the house is painted in a more subdued color scheme.

To emphasize the depth and three-dimensionality of a feature, paint the face one color and the underside surface in a shade of the same color.

In addition to picking out existing architectural features, consider using paint to add details where the architecture is very plain. A band of contrasting color carried all along the roofline can bring out the shape of the house and add interest to an otherwise featureless facade, much like sports striping on a car. In a similar fashion, plain trim can be made more visually complex by adding another color in a regular pattern, such as a stripe around the outside edge of all the window frames and doorframes.

Techniques for painting windows, doors, and trim are described on page 94.

Faux Finishes

The French word for false is *faux*. The original purpose of a faux finish was to imitate in paint the look of a more expensive building material. Some of the general techniques, such as sponged or mottled paint, have taken on a life of their own and are now used simply for their unique appearance.

Faux finishes, particularly marbleizing and wood graining, can be very time-consuming and exacting work for a beginner. Start by trying something very simple and direct. If the technique appeals to you and you find it easy, you can always apply a faux finish to some feature of the house after the basic painting is completed. Techniques for painting faux finishes are described on page 102.

Top: Think carefully about color choices for garage doors. A single door like this one can be painted in several colors without becoming overbearing. It is often better to paint large doors to blend with the house body. Notice the grout treatment.
Bottom: Houses with intricate trim lend themselves to fancy detailing.

Sponged Finishes

A sponged, or mottled, finish blends two or more colors directly on the surface to achieve the look of solid stone. It is the easiest of all the faux finishes and one of the most fun to do. It has one great advantage over other special effects: It can be used on a rough surface. In fact, rough surfaces really lend themselves to this technique.

Use colors that are similar in hue but not in value. Sponging will soften them, so that very dark colors can be used without looking heavy or oppressive. This process is suited to large areas, and especially to masonry surfaces, such as stucco, because the effect produced

is reminiscent of stone. Earth tones—ochres, umbers, and siennas—look the most natural in this context.

You can get interesting ideas for sponged surfaces by examining actual clay and rocks. When seen from up close, these natural formations often reveal many small spots of intense color. These blend together when viewed from a distance to give a more subdued overall effect. The variety of the individual colors gives visual interest and a sense of depth and complexity to natural building materials and to sponged surfaces alike.

When using a sponged finish on a wall, choose a contrasting

Top: You can bring out the details of a house without painting fancy trim. The lines of this modern stucco house are enhanced by subtle color variation.
Bottom: Faux finishes can mimic actual materials, or they can be purely imaginative. A simple modern house takes on a special character when painted with a flowing leaf motif.

color for the trim to increase the three-dimensional effect. An example would be a terra-cotta sponged finish on the house body and a shade of green for the trim.

Marbleizing

Paint can be used to imitate the colors, patterns, and veining of natural marble. This is an affordable way to add a touch of opulence to a house. Marbleizing looks more believable when it is applied to surfaces that could be made from real marble, such as a cornice, fascia, tympanum, doorsill, or column.

White, beige, yellow, red, green, blue, and black all occur naturally in marble. Whatever colors you choose, they must harmonize with the rest of the color scheme. A good way to get ideas for possible color combinations is to look at pieces of actual marble. Local marble distributors will have samples. You might also look at photographs in the library.

When planning keep in mind that marbleizing is more difficult to do on a curved surface, especially if the curves are intricate, and that, whatever its shape, the surface must be almost perfectly smooth.

Wood Graining

Paint can be used to imitate the colors and grain patterns of wood. Wood graining looks best on small areas, such as doors, doorjambs, windows, and window trim. Use it to give a natural-wood look to previously painted surfaces without the time-consuming and messy process of stripping the old finish. When planning keep in mind that wood graining, like marbleizing, is easiest to do on flat, smooth surfaces.

Wood graining can be used to make common construction materials resemble expensive and exotic woods. Quarter-sawed oak, bird's-eye maple, tiger skin mahogany, and a wide variety of tropical hardwoods are very beautiful and very costly. By substituting labor for materials, you can incorporate the look of these rare woods into the design of your house.

As with real wood, the colors used in graining should harmonize with the overall design. Check with lumberyards to find a local supplier of specialty woods. Use these to give yourself ideas.

Stenciling

You can produce an image or a pattern on any flat surface by painting through a stencil. This is a template cut out of thin material, usually cardboard or plastic. Stenciling is an inexpensive, imaginative, and exciting way to add individuality to a design. Ready-cut stencils are available at paint stores and hobby stores, or you can cut your own. Multiple colors can be used to define an intricate pattern. Use contrasting colors to call attention to stenciled designs. Experiment with different colors by stenciling the pattern onto paper first. Once you have the correct colors, tape the paper mock-up to the building to determine the correct placement.

Stencils are often used to create a pattern by repeating the same design over and over. Typical examples would be a pattern just below the roofline, around windows, or on the pillars of the front porch.

Stencils can also be used to create a single image. This is an effective way to alter the visual balance of a face of the house by drawing more attention to one part of it.

The simplest detailing, such as painting the trim pieces in contrast to the garage door, defines the house as one that has been designed rather than just painted.

Stenciling, seen here above the picture window and the doorway, is an easily mastered detailing technique. Stencils can be made by copying a pattern that occurs elsewhere on the house. Here the gable trim carving is repeated to the left of the window.

DESIGNING WITH WOOD STAINS AND SPECIALTY PRODUCTS

There is a wide variety of specialty products to consider in designing a color scheme. Stains and penetrating sealers bring out the natural beauty of wood. Varnishes protect the patina of metal and wood. Porch and deck paints protect heavy-traffic areas.

Stains and Penetrating Sealers

Natural stains make the least change in the color of the wood, because they have the least pigment. True natural stains are not used in exterior work, but the natural, or untinted, penetrating oil sealers perform the same aesthetic function. Although they must be renewed frequently, these products are the best choice for protecting and beautifying new natural wood.

Semitransparent stains have more pigment. They allow some of the natural color variations to show through, but contain enough pigment to push the color of the wood in one direction—toward red, toward blue, toward gray, and so forth. The pigment also helps to even out minor variations in the wood color. Semitransparent stain is a good choice for new rough surfaces, such as shingles or Texture 1-11 siding.

Opaque stains have enough pigment to make a solid color, but they still allow more of the natural texture of the surface to show through than does paint.

Like the semitransparent stains, opaque stains are available in a limited range of colors. Unlike semitransparent stains, opaque stains will cover all variations in the surface color of the wood. This makes them a good choice for previously stained wood that has weathered severely. Opaque stains also produce the lowest-gloss finish available to those parts of the country where flat oil paints are restricted.

Note that this classification is not absolute. Some companies offer products whose opacity falls between the categories given here.

Opposite: Stains come in a variety of colors and in different opacities. Here a red-tinted stain adds color to a wood-sided house while allowing the natural beauty of the grain to show through.
Above: Blue stain makes a wood house blend in with its environment.

The texture of the surface to be stained and its ability to absorb the product have a marked effect on the appearance of the finished work. Rough surfaces pick up and hold more pigment than smooth surfaces. Weathered wood is more absorbent than new wood. This is a major consideration in choosing stains. The less opaque the stain, the more pronounced the variations in color between absorbent or rough and nonabsorbent or smooth surfaces. This is a judgment call, but in general you should use a more heavily pigmented stain to mask unattractive variations.

For example, if you use a natural penetrating oil sealer, or even a semitransparent stain, on a wall covered with old, weathered shingles, and if there is a patch of new shingles in the middle of the wall, the difference in color between the old and new shingles will be nearly as great when you have finished staining as it was before. Even an opaque stain would not completely conceal the difference, but the more pigment there is in the stain, the less apparent that difference will be.

The pigment in exterior stain helps to block ultraviolet radiation from the sun, which attacks both the coating itself and exposed wood. This is so important that even so-called clear oil treatments for woodwork and decks contain a small amount of pigment.

As wood ages it develops a patina. You can see how the patina will be brought out by a clear finish by wetting the

Urethane preserves the natural color of wood siding while protecting it from the elements. Varnish is the traditional choice, but urethane is easier to apply.

46

surface with a damp cloth. (Be careful not to wet the wood too much or you will raise the grain.) If you find that color pleasing, a clear finish may be all you need. Keep in mind that a semitransparent stain will alter, but will not completely obscure, the color of the patina. The patina of wood is greatly influenced by moisture and sunlight. Applying a clear wood preservative to unpainted decks, rails, and shingles will help to preserve the patina and prevent the wood from fading and graying. Wood preservatives contain small quantities of pigment, which can help to even out blemishes and reduce graying on already weathered or damaged wood.

Some wood preservatives contain a small amount of gray pigment. Use these products to harmonize new wood with weathered wood.

Varnish and Urethane

If you want to preserve the color of natural wood or metal, but you also want to protect it, use a clear coating. Varnish and urethane are, respectively, the traditional and the modern choice. For mechanical reasons, varnish is usually preferable to urethane in exterior applications, but neither one is very durable. Varnish can be used to apply a clear, glossy finish to a natural-wood front door or to preserve the patina of weathered copper or the shine of polished brass.

Porch and Deck Paints

Steps, walkways, thresholds, porches, and decks cannot be painted with ordinary house paint if the coating is to last. Specially formulated porch and deck paints are available for these high-abrasion, heavy-traffic surfaces. Unfortunately, these products are available in a limited range of colors. Get samples of the colors at the paint store and work them into the color scheme.

Industrial enamels are a poor second best mechanically, but they can be used for areas that take heavy foot traffic, and they come in a much wider range of colors. Their drawback is that they must be frequently renewed.

Because porches and decks take a tremendous beating from snow, rain, and foot traffic, they require special paint, which comes in a limited range of colors. If you want the porch to match the house, make sure that the color you select is available in porch and deck paint as well as in house paint.

SHOPPING FOR SAMPLES

Good paint stores have thousands of colors, many gloss levels, and several qualities of paint from which to choose. The best procedure is to start by collecting samples. Take them home, test them around the house, and then decide on the final color scheme.

Local Knowledge

Knowledgeable sales staff are a wonderful source of good advice. They know which products are useful for the particular problems encountered in your area. The properties of paint and other finishing materials are discussed in this book in some detail (see page 78), but local advice is always valuable.

The paint store can also help in the design process. Along with materials, tools, and equipment, paint stores carry a wide selection of color samples, both on paper and in sample-sized cans. Most paint stores mix custom colors to specification, and many offer very good color-matching services.

Manufacturers' Color Samples

Every paint store features a display of color samples printed on card stock. Known as swatches, they contain between 5 and 10 samples per card, showing the relative values of a particular color. Each manufacturer preformulates between 1,200 and 2,000 basic colors, and all of these colors are shown on that manufacturer's sample cards.

Take as many samples as you think might be useful in determining a color scheme. Some manufacturers produce a complete set of cards, called a fan deck, which you can buy.

Selected colors will also be grouped on special charts. Among them may be historical colors; popular combinations; the colors available in specialty finishes, such as porch and deck paints; opaque and semitransparent stains; and metal paints.

Color Bases

Only a limited number of any manufacturer's formulated colors are actually mixed at the factory. Usually, these will be the colors that are currently in fashion. They are shown on separate color charts; sometimes they are also included in the fan deck.

The other colors have to be mixed at the paint store using the manufacturer's formulas. Most companies use a system of five different bases in which to mix their colors. The base with the least white pigment is used to mix both dark and pure colors.

Porch and deck paint, metal paints, and exterior stains are not available in all bases. Therefore certain colors may be impossible to duplicate in these product lines.

Tinting primers for dark finish coat colors require a deep-tone primer base. Most manufacturers make such a base, but not all paint stores stock it. It may have to be special-ordered. This may take several days, so plan ahead.

Factory-mixed colors are changed more frequently than the formulated colors. They cover slightly better than the colors that are mixed at the paint store.

Apply Samples to the House

Not many people can see color combinations in their heads. Use the sample cards to work out simple color schemes. For more complicated schemes start with the samples; then buy a small amount of each color and apply it directly to the house.

The object is to test the colors by putting them where they will ultimately go. To do this you will need buckets, brushes, paint-stirring sticks, and a drop cloth. Disposable paper buckets and disposable brushes are inexpensive and easy to clean up.

Set up by protecting the work area with a drop cloth and assembling the materials. Brush out each sample on the appropriate part of the house: body color on the body, trim color on the trim.

On the house the colors may look different than they looked on the card. Cover a large enough area to block out the previous color from the field of vision. This is important; the contrast with the existing color will alter the effect of the sample. Apply enough coats of paint so that none of the existing paint shows through. Since the amount of light will also affect the color, apply samples in both shady and sunny areas and view the results at different times of day.

Don't decide until the paint has completely dried. It will look different then. You can hasten the drying by using a blow dryer, but you will get a truer reading on the gloss level by allowing it to dry naturally. Latex paint should have reached its true color in an hour, perhaps less if the weather is warm and windy.

Save Color Formulas

Keep careful track of each color sample and list which elements of the house will be painted in each color. Use this list when you estimate how much paint you will need (see page 13). Once you have determined the color scheme, write down the name, number, and formula (including the proper base number) of each paint so that it can be mixed to specification. After purchasing the paint, keep the list in a safe place for future use. Some paint stores maintain formula files, but mistakes can happen, so it's safest to keep a copy for yourself.

More than anything else, the colors you choose for your house should reflect your personal style. If your taste runs to fun, you'll appreciate the combination of pink, blue, and yellow with purple accents that enlivens this little house.

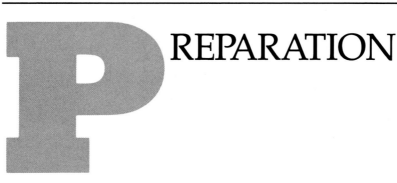

PREPARATION

Good preparation is the foundation of a good paint job. The best paint money can buy will not last long if it is applied over an unsound surface. With older houses this is where the bulk of the painter's time is often spent. Whether your house is old or new, good preparation can make your paint job look better and last longer. Identifying surface problems, knowing what needs to be done, deciding how much of it to do, and then getting the work accomplished are the subjects of this chapter.

Once the house is mechanically sound, the amount of additional preparation needed depends on the relative visibility of the area. Prepare a highly visible entrance, such as this blue front door, with more care than the less obviously visible second story.

UNDERSTANDING SURFACE CONDITIONS

Whether paint bonds properly depends primarily on the condition of the surface to which it is applied. If the surface is covered with oil or grime, the paint may not bond to it at all. If the surface of the old paint job is clean and dry but the old paint isn't sticking to the building anymore, the new paint won't be on the building long either.

Mechanical Reasons

The major objective of preparation is to make the surface to be painted free of dirt, grease, and loose material; dry; and mechanically sound. Every section in this chapter deals with some aspect of preparing for mechanical soundness.

Good preparation ensures that the new paint will adhere to the building. If it doesn't you will have to paint the house again in two years. If it does the paint will last for five years or more.

The amount of work it takes to prepare a house for painting depends on its condition. Start by doing an inspection (see page 54). Then follow these six steps to prepare for paint that will hold up in all weather conditions.

1. Remove everything that is unsound—dirt, grease, loose caulk, loose rust, loose glazing, rotten wood, and the rough, uneven edges of chipped paint—by washing, sanding, and stripping (see page 57).

2. Make all needed repairs, such as fixing large holes by patching (see page 68), caulking gaps between construction materials that allow moisture to get behind paint (see page 74), and repairing windows (see page 73).

3. Prime areas where stains may bleed through the finish coat, or where bare wood may rob patching materials of their binders, or where rust may develop.

4. Patch any holes or gaps where moisture may enter the structure or where surface imperfections allow water to stand. Patch rough areas to improve the appearance of the house.

5. Sand patches smooth and remove the dust made by all the preceding steps.

6. Prime any areas—including the new patches—that will absorb the finish coat at a different rate than the rest of the house.

The last parts of steps 1 and 4 could be extended indefinitely, or until the surface of the house was as smooth as a piece of furniture. Once mechanical soundness is achieved, all further preparation is done for reasons of appearance.

Reasons of Appearance

Preparation determines not only how long the paint job will last but also how it will

Old homes, such as this century-old Victorian, generally require more preparation than new ones. However, every house should be thoroughly inspected for surface problems prior to painting.

look. Absorbent surfaces—bare wood or a new patch—will dull the finish of gloss paints and in some cases can even change the appearance of flat finishes. Priming these areas helps keep the absorption rate of the finish coat even over the entire surface. Redwood and cedar have substances in them that are water soluble and can stain through latex paints. They must be sealed with an oil-based product before they can be painted with latex.

The higher the gloss of the finish, the more it shows every surface bump and ripple. Keep this in mind when you do the preparation. If the window frames are in bad shape and you don't want to do more than make them mechanically sound, consider using a lower-gloss finish, which will not call attention to the uneven surface. If the surface of a wall is irregular, consider applying the paint with a roller rather than a sprayer, because a sprayer follows the existing surface faithfully, whereas a roller adds its own slight texture. In some cases, it is even appropriate to roll on a coat of textured material to camouflage variations.

There is no limit to the amount of work you can do to improve the appearance of the surface. Eventually you will have to decide how much is enough. Keep in mind that what is visible from 2 feet away as you stand on a ladder may well be impossible to see from the ground.

The gloss level of the paint finish coat affects the amount of preparation needed. High-gloss paint, such as that used on this red front door, does not hide any surface problems. Because the door is so visible and takes abuse from weather and hard use, it requires special attention. Plan to sand and prime doors before painting them.

IDENTIFYING COMMON PROBLEMS

This section identifies common problems and their cause and explains briefly how to fix them. The rest of the chapter discusses repair procedures in detail. It also tells how to prevent these common problems from destroying the new paint job.

House Inspection

The first step in preparing the house for painting is to identify potential problems. Walk around the house and look closely at the condition of the surface. Sun and water are the great destroyers of paint jobs. Deterioration is likely to be greatest where the sun is hottest. On the opposite side of the house you may find mildew growing where the water is slow to evaporate.

Surface Dirt

Every house is dirty. At ground level, soil splashes onto the siding. Higher up, air pollution, car exhaust, and flying dust collect on the house body and on horizontal trim. All surface dirt must be washed off the entire house before priming and painting begins. If you plan to paint the house over several weeks, wash each section just several days before you start to paint it.

Oil and Grease

Anything oily will prevent paint from sticking. Remove oil and grease by scrubbing with detergent, waterblasting, sandblasting, or washing with solvents before priming and painting. Sometimes surface oil isn't noticeable until the wet paint starts to crawl away from the surface as it is applied. In such a case, if the area is small, sand the spot, wipe off the existing and fresh paint with a rag, and repaint immediately. If this doesn't work, wait for the paint to dry, scrape it off, and prepare that part over.

Chalking

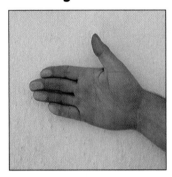

The binders that hold the paint together gradually break down. The result is a film of pigment on the surface that looks like a layer of chalk dust. It is not always obvious that a surface is chalking, so test it by running your hand across it; see if you pick up a layer of residue. Like surface dirt, chalking paint must be washed off before priming and painting.

Mildew

If you find black spots or black or green stains, you have mildew. The spots are colonies of small organisms that need moisture and heat to thrive. Kill surface mildew by washing with a chlorine bleach solution before priming and painting.

Metal Stains

Iron and copper railings, flashing, and fixtures form water-soluble oxides, which drip onto wood surfaces, forming reddish brown or black stains. Wash the stains off the wood before priming and painting. To prevent them from recurring, prime the metal properly before you paint it. If you like the look of weathered copper and the patina is relatively sound, but you don't want stains washing onto the body of the house, seal the metal with a clear coating when you put the finishing touches on the project.

Rot

Dry rot (dry, crumbly remnants of wood) and wet rot (soggy soft spots) are organic infestations like mildew. Rot destroys the wood so completely that you can push your finger right into it. Wood is susceptible to rot wherever it remains wet. To prevent rot make sure that the wood is well protected against water.

All the old rot should be removed, or the rot should be killed with a biocide designed for that purpose, before the hole is patched. If this is not done, the rot may continue to grow behind the patch. Stabilize the remaining damaged wood with a resinous wood hardener. Patch the hole with resin fillers.

Termites

These insects eat wood. They tunnel through it like carpenter ants, but unlike ants, termites can destroy a wood frame house if left unchecked. Termites enter the structure where wood is in contact with the ground. If you suspect that any part of the house is infested with termites, get a professional to inspect it and destroy them if necessary before you do anything else.

Wood Dyes

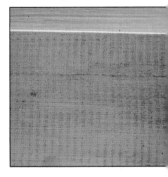

Redwood, cypress, and red cedar contain natural dyes that will bleed through latex paint and through tiny cracks in oil paint, causing a brownish stain on the surface. To prevent this from happening, seal the wood with an oil-based primer.

Yellow pine and the knots of some other softwoods have a high resin content. If the wood is new, the resins may still be seeping when the wood is painted. This will lift and discolor oil or latex paint. The solution is to spot-prime all knots with a pigmented shellac to seal out the resin.

Nail Holes

Fill these with exterior spackling compound or linseed oil putty. There is no need to prime an empty hole before patching. If you are patching over the heads of nails that have been countersunk, seal them first with shellac. Not only will this keep rusting nail heads from staining through but it will also make the patching material adhere better.

Tear Out

Caused by milling processes, tear out is sometimes found in new trim or wood railings. It looks like a series of tiny chisel gouges. As long as tear out is not in a place where it can collect water, there is no mechanical reason to patch it, but there may be an aesthetic reason. Tear out cannot be removed except by patching. Use exterior spackling compound, linseed oil putty, or a resin filler. It is important to prime shallow imperfections like this before filling them with putty or spackling compound. The primer prevents the wood from soaking up the binders and solvents in the patching material and weakening it by drying it too fast. If the material is an absorbent compound, the finished patch must also be sealed to prevent flashing (uneven gloss) in the finish coat.

Uneven or Chipped Paint

Ideally, imperfections in the existing paint should be dealt with by sanding or stripping the old paint back to a smooth surface. As a matter of practice, it is hard to resist the temptation to patch them instead. Even if you decide to patch instead of strip, remove the loose paint and get back to a sound surface of bare wood or masonry and firmly attached paint. Prime before patching here, since the imperfections tend to be broad and shallow, making patching materials particularly vulnerable to movement in the substrate. It is difficult to make these patches perfectly smooth when they are first applied, so it is best to use exterior spackling compound and sand it to a smooth surface.

Cracks

Repair small cracks with flexible materials, such as caulk. This includes cracks in wood siding or trim, cracks or gaps between different kinds of building material, and small cracks in stucco. Large cracks should be repaired with stucco patch. The cracks should be at least ½ inch wide in order to admit enough patch to make a durable repair. Small amounts of stucco patch are not stable. If you want to patch deep or wide cracks in wood, use resin fillers. Other patching materials will not hold in something that moves as much as a crack in wood.

Cracked Window Glazing

The surface of the glazing compound may be alligatored if the putty was applied in direct sun on a hot day, or if it was painted too soon after it was applied. If the glazing compound is still soundly attached to the window and sash but its surface is covered with shallow cracks, this is more a cosmetic problem than a mechanical one. Simply add new glazing compound to fill the cracks.

Occasionally, the glazing compound will be badly cracked and much of it will come off with a little scraping, but a substantial amount will still be stuck to the sash. This window could be reglazed as it is, going over the old tightly attached putty, but it is better to get back to a clean sash by stripping with heat before reglazing.

Alligatoring and Crazing

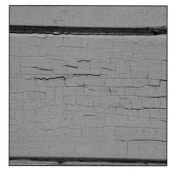

Both alligatoring and crazing (also called checking) occur when the surface paint dries faster than it should, causing it to crack. This usually happens where a fast-drying finish coat has been applied (perhaps in direct sun on a hot afternoon) over a coat of slow-drying paint. Alligatoring is also caused by putting on too thick a coat of paint. Instead of drying like paint, it dries like mud on the bottom of a puddle. Crazing can occur if a single coat of paint dries too quickly, as it might in very hot sun.

Wait for each coat of paint to dry to prevent these problems from happening in the future. To remove alligatoring and crazing, scrape and sand the affected area, or patch it smooth, or both before priming and painting.

Blistering

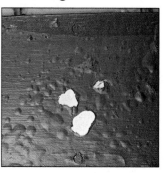

Moisture trying to escape from behind the paint causes most blistering. Surfaces that are kept wet from behind (for example, a bathroom window) are particularly vulnerable. Blistering can be aggravated by poor adhesion caused by painting over surface dirt.

Like peeling, blistering is prevented by keeping moisture out from behind the paint. To remove blistering paint scrape and sand to a sound, smooth surface before priming and painting.

Peeling

Blistering and peeling are the most obvious paint failures. Peeling happens when the surface on which the paint was laid changes shape and the paint cannot keep up. Boards swell and shrink with changes in temperature and moisture content. Within certain limits the paint film is flexible, but when those limits are exceeded, the paint cracks. This aggravates the changes in the wood by allowing more moisture to enter, and the cycle accelerates. Winter snow and ice can also contribute to peeling, especially near areas of the roof where ice dams form. The roof drainage is overtaxed, shingles and clapboards are lifted or displaced, and water seeps in behind the wall.

The only way to prevent paint from peeling is to keep moisture from entering behind it. Thin paint films are more flexible than very thick ones. Paint is also less likely to peel if it is well anchored to the surface.

To remove peeling paint scrape and sand to a sound, smooth surface before priming and painting.

All old, peeling paint, whether on horizontal board siding (top) or on metal (bottom), must be removed so that the new paint will adhere to the surface properly.

Knotholes

It is difficult to patch knotholes successfully because there is very little for the patch to hold onto and many forces at work to pop it back out. If the holes are small enough, they can be patched with a plug of resin filler. In extreme cases it may be necessary to nail a piece of aluminum flashing over the hole. If the flashing is properly primed and caulked, this makes a very sound mechanical solution. The aesthetics may leave something to be desired, but unless you are willing to keep repairing the same area over and over, this may be the best you can do.

If the hole is in a thick piece of wood (such as a windowsill), the outlook for a successful patch is better. In this case, use a resin filler.

Holes in Stucco

A hole larger than 1 inch in diameter can be filled with stucco patch. A slightly smaller hole can also be filled with stucco patch, but it shouldn't be filled quite up to the surface. The last bit of space can be filled with a flexible patching compound. This should be spread out around the hole to make a good seal and to give the compound a larger surface to grip. Smaller holes should be treated just like cracks in stucco and patched with caulk or other flexible material.

Holes in Masonry

Holes in cinder block or cement block can be patched, but they have to be backed up first, or the patching material will simply fall down inside the hollow block.

To do this, cut wire mesh or hardware cloth larger than the hole. Attach a string to the middle of the mesh. Push the mesh into the hole and pull gently on the string to keep it in place. Consider using expanding urethane foam rather than stucco patch, especially if the wall of the block is thin.

Holes in the porous surface of cinder block and cement blocks or bricks are filled with a special class of primers called block fillers. These fillers are designed to fill small voids in a single coat, leaving the surface ready to be painted.

Treat holes in other kinds of masonry like holes in stucco.

Holes in Metal

Small holes in gutters or aluminum window frames can cause big problems of water leakage. If the metal is clean and dry, holes up to the size of a nail hole can be patched with caulking compound. Even the best solvent-based caulking compounds do not stick very well to metal, however, so this must be viewed as a quick fix. For a permanent solution try one of the epoxy products designed specifically for patching metals. For larger holes in painted or bare metal gutters and downspouts, rivet or solder in a patch.

CLEANING THE SURFACE

The house painter has a variety of methods to get the house into good shape for painting. Many potential problems admit of more than one solution. This section describes the method best suited to your needs, as well as to your ability, time, and patience.

Washing

The best way to remove surface dirt and chalking is to wash the house by hand or with a high-pressure pumping unit called a waterblaster.

Whichever method you use, finish all of the washing before you start sanding, priming, or painting. Water is the greatest destroyer of paint jobs, so allow plenty of drying time.

Washing away mildew is a special case. The technique is outlined below.

Hand Washing

To wash down the building by hand, use a solution of trisodium phosphate (TSP) or other strong detergent. Use a scrub brush with a handle to protect your hands and so that you won't have to move the ladder often. Use a pothook to hang the bucket from the ladder to keep your hands free. Use a pistol grip nozzle for the hose to conserve water. Spray plants below you from time to time to keep the detergent from building up on the leaves. Wear rubber gloves and eye protection and be cautious about working over your head.

Work from the top of the building down, finishing one side of the house at a time. Thoroughly clean horizontal surfaces, on which dirt may have built up.

Waterblasting

A waterblaster or pressure washer is a gasoline-powered pump that takes the normal pressure from a garden hose and boosts it, sending it out through a fan tip at the end of a pistol grip wand at a pressure of 1,500 to 2,500 psi. These pressures remove chalking paint and surface dirt as well as some loose paint. A waterblaster will remove loose paint very well from stiff surfaces, such as brick and stucco, and fairly well from flexible surfaces, such as wood.

Tool rental establishments and some paint and hardware stores rent waterblasters. If washing off surface dirt and caulking paint is all that is required, a small unit will do. If there is a great deal of peeling paint to be removed from masonry surfaces, rent a larger unit capable of producing higher water pressure.

High-pressure jets of water can be dangerous. Do not point the waterblaster at unprotected skin. The high pressure can cause a puncture wound, which can easily become infected. The chips flying off the building can come at considerable speed. Wear rubber gloves and eye protection when using a waterblaster.

Waterblasting

Goggles

Spray nozzle

Spray wand

Rain gear

Gloves

Water supply hose

Gas-powered machine

The more powerful water-blasters can easily gouge wood or break window glass, so aim carefully. Avoid playing the jet of water on doors and windows, particularly on the sills and frames. Houses are designed to withstand rain falling from above, not high-pressure jets coming from all angles. Check the inside of the house from time to time (even if you are being careful) to catch any water that may have come in around windows or doors. This is more important for older buildings, which are not built as tightly as modern ones. Protect particularly vulnerable areas, such as wallpaper or natural paneling, by placing a towel on the inside sill of the window or door to absorb any stray leaks.

If there is loose paint, the chips will be flying thick and fast. Use burlap or old bed sheets as drops to save time in cleaning up paint chips from the lawn and flower beds. Sheets make poor drop cloths for painting, because they are so light that the paint soaks right through. However, that is an advantage in this case. Sheets are light even when soaking wet, and they dry out quickly, allowing you to shake off and sweep up the chips for disposal.

Be careful working from a ladder with a waterblaster. The spray wand starts and stops with a bit of a kick, and it can throw you off balance if you are not ready for it.

All this may make water-blasting sound difficult. It is not. It is much faster than doing the job by hand, is by far

the best way to prepare masonry surfaces, and is quite safe if you observe the precautions.

To waterblast a house connect a garden hose to the waterblaster water intake, connect the high-pressure hose to the outlet on the waterblaster, and connect the spray wand to the other end of the high-pressure hose. Select a fan tip from the assortment that is supplied with the waterblaster and connect it to the end of the spray wand. Turn on the water to the hose. Start the gasoline engine of the waterblaster according to the manufacturer's instructions. Remove material by moving the wand back and forth to play the jet of water evenly over the surface of the house. Experiment to find the correct distance from the building and the best fan width.

Removing Mildew

If mildew is painted over, it will grow behind and eventually through the fresh paint. Before you paint you need to kill the mildew and remove the residue. The best way to do this is to wash it off, using a solution of chlorine bleach and detergent in water. The bleach kills the mildew, and the detergent helps to remove the residue. There are several proprietary products on the market that work very well, but nearly the same results can be obtained with a home brew of soapy water and bleach in proportions of 3 to 1. Use a strong detergent, such as TSP.

If you are washing the house by hand, simply add the bleach to the water bucket. Wet the plants before you start using bleach around them and rinse them off when you rinse the walls. If you have a severe mildew problem, it's a good idea to use a stronger commercial product. The time you save will be worth the money.

If you are waterblasting, apply the soapy water and bleach, or a commercial preparation, to each area before you wash it down. Use a bucket and brush or a garden sprayer. Waterblast after the solution has had 15 minutes to work, or follow the manufacturer's directions.

Mildew will grow in any place that is warm, damp, and shady, and there is, finally, not much you can do to prevent it. If you decide to try to remove mildew without intending to repaint, be very careful. Bleach and strong detergents can dull the paint finish.

Scraping

Often the best way to remove loose paint, particularly where the shape of the surface or proximity of window glass makes sanding difficult, is to scrape it. Scraping is also the best approach where the existing paint is loosely attached to the surface or where the finish has become gummy.

Hand Scraping

There are two basic types of scraper. Pull-models have a blade set at right angles to the handle. They are used with two hands, pressing the blade against the surface and pulling

the scraper toward you. Push-models resemble chisels or stiff putty knives; the blade is set in line with the handle. You lift the edge of the paint by pushing the blade under it.

One class of scraper deserves particular mention. Molding scrapers are pull models with curved blades designed to fit into the grooves and curlicues of millwork, such as window trim. If you have a lot of loose paint in the hard-to-get-at shapes on the trim of your house, it is well worthwhile to find the appropriate molding scrapers.

The first rule when scraping is to avoid gouging the wood. The best way to do this is to work with the grain rather than against it or across it. Even relatively small gouges across the grain of the wood will show from some distance. The eye is a little more forgiving of scratches that go with the grain. Be particularly careful when using a flat-bladed push scraper to get under the old paint. It's easy to forget the grain of the wood and tear out a sizable chunk of windowsill, especially when you're pushing along an outside corner.

Scraping is vigorous exercise, and it can put unaccustomed strain on the muscles. When working on a ladder, especially, you will find yourself using your lower back muscles a lot. Go easy at first, take breaks, and switch jobs and positions frequently.

Scraping

Scrape in direction
of wood grain

Goggles

Dust mask

Gloves

Pull-model scraper

Scrapers

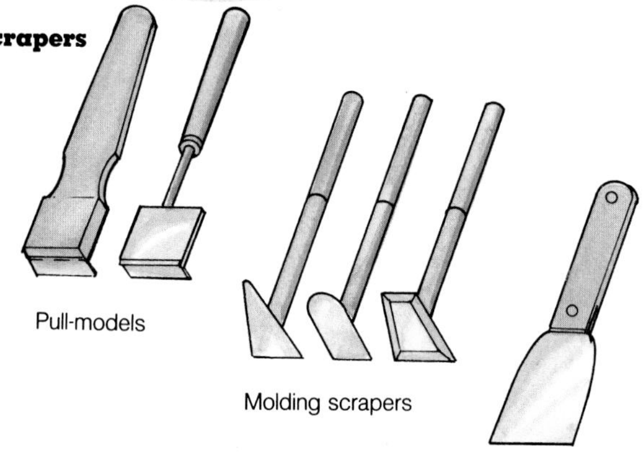

Pull-models

Molding scrapers

Push-model

Stripping

An advanced method of scraping, stripping uses heat or chemicals to remove all of the paint and get back to the original surface. It is used to reveal all the details of a carved piece or to prepare previously painted surfaces for staining. How far you go in stripping depends on what finish you intend to use. If you want to repaint, you are primarily interested in the shape and soundness of the surface. If you want to stain and varnish, however, you must remove all of the existing paint or stain. Before you set your heart on staining an old piece of painted woodwork, remember that there may be patched areas under that paint. If there are, you may get better results by repainting, since the patches will not take stain in anything like the same manner as the wood.

Heat Stripping

As paint heats up, it becomes soft and gummy. This makes it easy to scrape off. Heat will soften latex paint, but it works best on oil. There is no better, faster way to take many layers of paint off a curved surface than with heat and a scraper. Heat doesn't work very well on masonry and thick metal. These substances absorb the heat too quickly. Wood is a better insulator, so it lets the paint absorb the heat.

Heat can be dangerous. The trick is to apply just enough of it to soften the paint but not enough to ignite it or to scorch the wood underneath.

For many years blowtorches were used for stripping. Today they have been replaced by heat guns. Heat guns cost 5 to 10 times as much as a good brush and can be purchased at paint and hardware stores. Sometimes you can find them at tool rental establishments.

A heat gun is really a glorified blow dryer that achieves very high temperatures. Although it is safer than a blowtorch, it can still start a fire. Be extremely careful in using heat. Always wear gloves and a mask to protect yourself from the fumes (particularly if you are working in a confined space, such as a porch). Use the right scrapers for the job and have a bucket handy to collect the scrapings. They may be too hot to handle when they are first removed. Cover the ground with a drop cloth.

Do not use heat to strip if you cannot be around for a few hours after you finish the job. Never, never let the heat play on an opening into the inside of the wall. Inside the wall of every frame house is a tar paper vapor barrier. There may also be old newspapers that someone used to fill a hole before they plastered it years ago. That paper is now dry tinder. If a fire does start inside a wall, you may not notice it until it is too late.

To avoid burning the surface you are trying to strip, keep the heat gun moving. Watch the effect you are having on the paint and on the wood. It takes a little while to soften the paint. You don't

Stripping

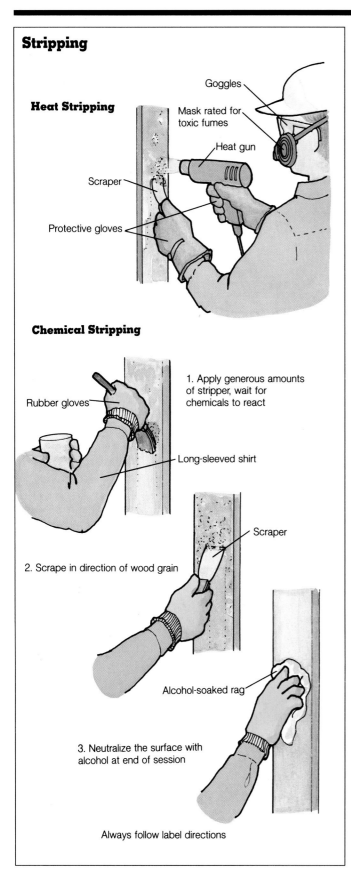

Heat Stripping

Goggles

Mask rated for toxic fumes

Heat gun

Scraper

Protective gloves

Chemical Stripping

Rubber gloves

1. Apply generous amounts of stripper, wait for chemicals to react

Long-sleeved shirt

Scraper

2. Scrape in direction of wood grain

Alcohol-soaked rag

3. Neutralize the surface with alcohol at end of session

Always follow label directions

have to be right on top of it to make it work. Eventually, you will begin to see that if you hold the heat gun a few inches from the surface, moving it back and forth over a small area, the paint will be soft enough to scrape in just a few moments. Scrape as directed (see page 58). Keep the heat gun in one hand and the scraper in the other and slowly move along the surface to be stripped. Later you can sand the little bit of residue left behind.

Scorched wood accepts paint poorly. If you do happen to scorch the wood badly enough to char it, use a stain killer to hold out the stains and hold onto the now very hard surface. If it is deeply charred, remove the charred material, prime the area, and patch the gouge.

Chemical Stripping

Chemical strippers lift the old paint layer by layer. This is the best way to prepare previously painted surfaces for transparent stains and for varnishing.

Although they are fast acting and quick to use, chemical strippers are caustic and toxic. Avoid contact with skin and eyes and prolonged breathing of vapors. Follow the directions on the label carefully. Wear a long-sleeved shirt, long pants, rubber gloves, and eye protection. Wear a mask rated for toxic fumes when working in a confined space.

Most strippers are alkaline, some extremely so. Check the label to determine the proper neutralizer and keep it handy in case a drop of the stripper gets on your skin.

Along with the chemical stripper, have scrapers that will fit into the detailing; a metal bucket to hold the stripper; a throw-away bristle brush with which to apply the stripper (or a spray bottle, if the stripper is liquid enough); a bucket to hold the scrapings; a small, stiff brush to get into the details; plenty of alcohol and steel wool with which to scrape residue; and a good drop cloth or layers of paper to protect the area beneath you and to make cleanup easy.

The amount of stripper needed depends on how many layers of paint there are to remove. Start with a quart and take a representative section down to bare wood. See how much stripper has been used and how large an area remains to be stripped. Judge from that how much will be needed to complete the project.

Chemical strippers are indiscriminate in their action. If a stray drop falls on a coated surface, it will lift the finish faster than you can say, "Oh no!" The best prevention is to mask well, use drop cloths, and be ready to refinish surfaces adjacent to the area you are stripping.

To use chemical stripper start by coating a small area. Don't be stingy; this isn't paint. Put on as much as possible without having the stripper run all over. Wait about 10 minutes for the stripper to react, or follow the container directions. The surface of the paint will begin to bubble and wrinkle. Before the stripper starts to dry out, scrape off the softened mess and put it in the collection bucket.

Apply more stripper, this time to a wider area. The aim is to scrape one section while the next one is still bubbling and wrinkling. Cover as much as you can scrape conveniently in 10 or 15 minutes. Don't get too far ahead with applying the stripper. When it dries out its effects begin to reverse, and the paint hardens up again. If more stripper is then applied, it will not work well.

Use the stiff brush or a knife point to get the last bits of old paint out of the curls and corners of detailed trim.

To end a chemical-stripping session, either for the day or for good, remove the last bits of stripper and softened paint or varnish and neutralize the surface. Either water or alcohol will neutralize most strippers, but always use alcohol to neutralize the stripper on the surface of woodwork. Water will be absorbed by the wood and raise the grain. Alcohol is also a solvent for paints and stains and can be used to remove the last traces of old material from the wood. Steel wool and alcohol is the final treatment for wood that is being readied for restaining.

Paste Strippers

There is another kind of chemical stripper that is much less toxic than the types described above. Slow-acting paste strippers are mildly caustic, like a strong hand soap. They are used as follows.

Apply a layer of paste to the surface to be stripped. Leave it there for 24 to 36 hours. If possible, cover the pasted area with plastic to keep it from drying out. When the time is up, scrape off the paste and softened paint. If hard paint remains, repeat the process. Remove the final remnants with alcohol and steel wool. Although this method is slow, it requires no special precautions, making it the safest choice available.

Sanding

In painting, a surface may be sanded either to smooth it or to rough it up. In exterior painting most sanding is done to remove surface problem material, such as weathered wood, chipped paint, and excess patch. It is also done to take the gloss off sound, clean surfaces so that the new paint will adhere to them.

Sandpaper, sanding disks, and sanding belts are graded according to the coarseness of the grit. The coarser the grit, the smaller the number. For exterior painting use 100 grit for fine work, 80 grit for medium work, and 60 grit or smaller for coarse work. The coarser papers will remove material faster and last longer without clogging up, but they can leave scratches. Remember that scratches show more clearly across the grain than with the grain, and that gloss paint shows surface defects more than flat paint. If a critical area is scratched, sand it with a finer grit or patch over it.

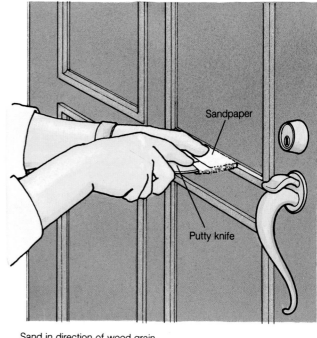

Hand Sanding Details

Sandpaper

Putty knife

Sand in direction of wood grain

For small areas or intricate surfaces, use a folded piece of sandpaper or wrap a piece around a block of wood or putty knife.

For large areas or when a lot of material must be removed, consider using an electric sander. There are several types available.

Orbital or vibrating sanders, also called block sanders, are the easiest for a novice to use without leaving deep scratches. They do not remove material as quickly as other electric sanders, so the danger of leaving ripples is also less.

Belt sanders remove material more quickly than orbital sanders. Be careful not to hold them in one spot so long that they cut a furrow in the wood. Because the abrasives move in a straight line, however, it is relatively easy to keep any scratches going with the grain.

Rotary sanders (or electric drills rigged with sanding disks to imitate them) can remove material very quickly, but they are temperamental to use. Because the abrasive material moves in a circle, these sanders leave swirl marks. Because they cut so fast and can't be held exactly perpendicular to the work surface, it is also very easy to leave ripples. These may not be obvious in bare wood, but they will be very obvious in a uniformly painted surface, especially if you use gloss paint.

It might seem reasonable simply to use a fine grit of sandpaper and so avoid leaving swirl marks or ripples. However, fast-moving abrasives

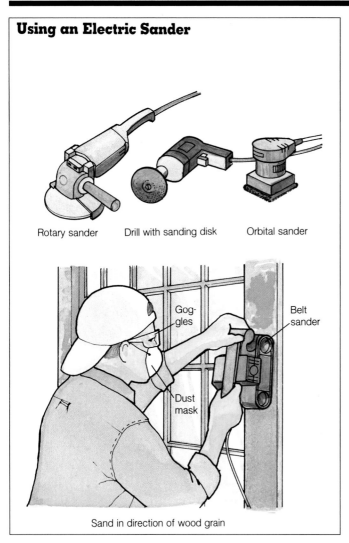

Using an Electric Sander

Rotary sander   Drill with sanding disk   Orbital sander

Goggles

Belt sander

Dust mask

Sand in direction of wood grain

create heat, and the heat softens the paint. The softened paint sticks to the surface of the sandpaper, rendering it useless. Stop using the disk when it gets clogged with paint. The finer the grit, the faster this happens.

Sanders are most often used in exterior painting to feather out areas where chipped paint has been removed. The object is to smooth the sharp edges of these areas so that they blend into the surrounding surface. The key to doing this well is to realize that wood is much softer than dried paint. You will cut away more of the wood in half a second than you will

of the dried paint in three seconds. Sand the paint. Don't touch the wood.

The trick to using belt and rotary sanders, especially for the novice, is to use them sparingly. Just take off the bulk of the material. Then do the finish work by hand or with an orbital sander.

Sanders are available at tool rental establishments for a small fee. If you have an electric drill, buy a sanding-disk adapter for it. Some sanding disks are held in place by a specially shaped washer; others have a gummed back. Each requires its own type of adapter.

The disks must be the same size as the backing pad. A little overhang is good, but if there is too much, the edge of the disk will quickly catch and tear (or try to tear the grinder out of your hands).

All sanding makes dust, and electric sanders fling it around at high speed. Always wear goggles and a dust mask when you sand. Finish all the sanding in an area (like a side of the house) before you do any priming or painting there. Watch the power cord when the disk is moving, particularly with rotary sanders. The edge of the disk can cut the insulation before you know it. Be careful.

Preparing Metal Surfaces

Unless they are coated with a factory finish of vinyl or baked-on enamel, metal surfaces require special preparation. Each type of metal has its own requirements. If metal surfaces are to be painted, they should be primed as soon after preparation as possible to prevent corrosion (see page 54).

Iron and Steel

Nails, screws, bolts, decorative work, braces for window frames and doorframes, the window frames themselves, some doors, hinges, and fire escapes are usually made of iron or steel. Iron and steel oxidize to form rust when they are exposed to water, and especially to salt water. An iron railing will often have bubbles along it where pinholes in the paint and primer allowed water to enter. As the rust forms,

it expands, pushing up the paint and allowing more water to collect. Because the paints used for coating metals are somewhat tougher than wood paints, they may continue to form a shell over the growing rust for some time. This is why it is important to scrape metal throughly prior to painting. What appears from a distance to be sound may not be.

The primary object in painting iron and steel is to protect it from moisture. For the paint to stick properly, any rust that is not firmly attached to the metal must be removed before the metal is primed. Chisel-style scrapers and wire brushes are the best tools for removing old rust. Scrape down the loose paint and the larger rust deposits with the chisel, and remove the residue with the brush. In some circumstances a wire brush attachment to an electric drill may be useful, but be careful: The brush can catch and wrench the drill from your hands. Always wear goggles and a dust mask when you use this attachment.

When all the loose rust has been removed, the metal is ready for priming. Prime iron and steel immediately after preparation to prevent further rusting. Use special primers designed for rusty metal.

New iron and steel can also be rusty. Treat them as described above. In addition, new metal can have mill oil or mill scale on it. The oil should be removed with naphtha or other solvent just before priming. Scale is a product of milling; scrap or chisel it off before priming and painting. Use bright-metal primers for unrusted steel and iron.

Preparing Metal Surfaces

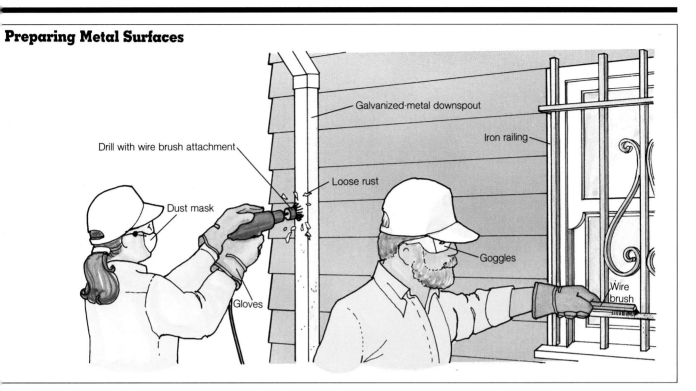

Drill with wire brush attachment

Dust mask

Gloves

Loose rust

Galvanized-metal downspout

Iron railing

Goggles

Wire brush

Galvanized Metal

Gutters, downspouts, and flashing around roofs, windows, and doors are commonly made of galvanized steel. This is steel with zinc coating. The zinc starts out very bright and silvery. As it weathers it turns a dull gray.

Traditional galvanized metal must be etched with a mild solution of phosphoric acid or acetic acid before being primed. Phosphoric acid, also called metal etch, is sold in paint and hardware stores. Follow the directions and cautions on the label. Acetic acid is simply distilled vinegar. Etching removes the residual mill oil from the surface of the metal. It also gives it a little tooth. After you have etched the metal, prime it with green or yellow zinc chromate primer. Galvanized-steel primers of the newer emulsion type eliminate the need to etch the metal.

If the galvanized product has weathered, it will already have been etched by the slight oxidation of the surface of the zinc. Weathered metal can be primed directly with oil-based or water-based galvanized-metal primers. If it has been exposed to the weather for so long that the zinc is corroded through and the steel behind it is beginning to rust, treat it like rusty metal.

In preparing previously painted galvanized-metal surfaces, avoid sanding or any other method that will scratch through the zinc coating to expose the steel. The zinc does more to protect the steel than the paint will.

Aluminum

Window frames, screen doors, and many decorative items are made from aluminum. Aluminum is treated like galvanized metal, except that etching is not necessary. The same primers are appropriate.

When raw aluminum is exposed to the weather, it develops a protective coating of oxides, which slows further corrosion. Where the atmosphere is very corrosive—at the beach, for example—even aluminum must be protected by paint. The natural oxides of aluminum make a good foundation for the primer. If the corrosion is very rough, smooth it down before you paint by sanding it lightly.

Anodized aluminum has a factory finish that gives it color, often some version of bronze. Treat it in the same way as other aluminum.

Copper and Brass

Like aluminum, brass and copper form their own protective coating of oxides. Therefore, they do not need paint to protect them. Copper used for gutters or screens may leave stains where water washes the oxide coating onto another surface. Bright copper and brass can be coated with exterior varnish to prevent them from oxidizing, but the varnish does not weather well and must be renewed frequently. To paint copper or brass, prime them first with oil-based metal primers. Water-based primers will not prevent oxide stains from forming.

To clean old paint from brass, remove the object and soak it in ammonia. This will lift the old paint in a matter of hours. A weak solution of nitric acid will remove corrosion from copper. In both cases, be sure to rinse the surface well with clean water to remove the residual acid or ammonia.

# PRIMING

Primer has many purposes. It adheres to the surface of the building and provides a surface for the next coat to adhere to. It protects the material being coated and seals the surface to keep chemicals in the material from staining the finish coat. In addition, primer prevents flashing by evening out any differences in the ability of the surface to absorb the next coat.

Primer Rules

Each primer is designed for specific applications. A good paint store should have personnel who are familiar with the common building materials and weather conditions in your area and with the primers best suited to those materials and conditions. Here are some rules that apply to all primers.

Primer is paint. Rules of dropping and masking (see page 24), setting up (see page 20), using equipment (see page 16), and application apply to priming as well as to painting. However, some other rules are unique to primers.

Tinting

Unlike paints primers are optimized for their function, not for their looks. Some primers come in only one color. Many have so much white in them that they cannot be tinted to match dark colors. Nevertheless, whenever possible, you should tint primer to approximate the color that will be painted over it. This will help the paint to cover in a single finish coat, saving you time and effort. Do not tint the primer to match the finish coat exactly. If the color of the dry primer is too close to that of the wet finish coat, you will have a devil of a time making sure that you have covered all of it. You may easily end up with holidays, the fanciful term for a missed spot in a coat of paint.

Timing

The drying time, the time between coats, is important. Some primers dry in a matter of days, some in a matter of minutes. Some primers can remain exposed to the weather for weeks; others must be finish-coated within days. Nearly all primers deteriorate more quickly than paint. If linseed oil primer is left to cure for too long, its surface will become so hard that the finish coat will not adhere properly. In other words, it will cease to be a good primer. Consult the manufacturer's directions or ask knowledgeable sales personnel for details. As a general rule, the faster the primer dries, the less time it will last when exposed to the weather and the more quickly it will become too hard to make a good surface for the next coat. Plan the project accordingly.

Some primers can be applied and finish-coated the same day. A few need several days to cure sufficiently. Many need 24 hours. Check the label for the manufacturer's recommendations.

Quick-Drying Primers

Primers that dry fast are usually solvent based. They dry quickly because they use such volatile solvents as alcohols and naphtha. Pigmented shellacs are of this type. Some quick-drying metal primers are epoxies.

Quick-drying primers are most useful in exterior painting as stain killers and sealers. Pigmented shellac will hold back wood resin stains that bleed through regular oil-based primers.

Quick-drying primers really come in handy when you discover that you left one spot unprimed just as you are about to start applying the finish coat. You can prime that one spot and go to the next window (or have a cup of coffee); by the time you get back to it, the primer will be dry enough to paint over. However, remember that the faster a primer dries, the less time it can be exposed to weather. The super-fast-drying primers are not weather resistant even under the finish coat. This is because they are very brittle and can not expand and contract with the house. Using them here and there is one thing; using them to hold back difficult stains is necessary; but using them for the whole house—or even for a large area—is a bad idea.

Some quick-drying primers clean up with paint thinner. Others clean up with alcohol or lacquer thinner. Check the recommendations on the label.

Wood Primers

These primers penetrate the surface of the wood; they seal it so that the next coat will be absorbed evenly and so that dyes, resins, and oils in the wood will not leach into the finish coat.

Oil-Based Wood Primers

Oil-based primers make an excellent foundation for the next coat of paint; they do a great job of holding out stains of various kinds; and, unlike latex primers, they stick to moderately dirty or chalking surfaces. Their greatest weakness (apart from the fact that they are a little more trouble to clean up) is that the surface must be dry before it is primed with oil. Oil-based primers form an impermeable vapor barrier. Any moisture underneath the primer will lift the primer right off the building when the water turns to vapor in the sun.

Their combined strengths and weaknesses make oil-based primers the best choice for anything that has been painted before. Good-quality oil-based wood primers make fair all-purpose primers. They will cling to ill-prepared surfaces for a little while longer than latex primers would. However, sloppy preparation will show sooner or later, no matter what kind of primer is used.

Latex Wood Primers

Latex primers are easier to work with than oil-based primers; they dry faster; and they are more forgiving of some residual moisture in the wood. However, they have their disadvantages. Although the newer ones hold out stains better, they are still weaker in this respect than oils. Also, many species of pine and fir, especially southern yellow pine, contain resins related to turpentine. This is not a problem with oil-based primers, but it can prevent latex primers from adhering.

Except where staining is a problem, latex is the preferred primer for new wood.

Latex primers are still subject to flash rusting. That is, the water and certain chemicals in the paint can speed the rusting of bare metal, such as nail heads. The rust seeps into the wet paint, making a stain on the surface. Not only does this look ugly, but the rust will continue to grow and eventually push the paint off the building. The solution is to wait for the latex to dry and then prime the stains with a quick-drying primer. This will stop the rust from growing.

Some latex primers include alkyd-modified resins in suspension. These primers may show rust stains, but the rust is safely trapped in the surface of the primer. No further staining should occur.

Stucco and Masonry Primers

All primers designed for use on stucco and masonry must seal off any chemicals on or near the surface. They must also provide a new surface with an even rate of absorption for the next coat. In addition, special masonry primers are available to deal with specific problems.

Latex Masonry Primers

Sometimes masonry will have hot spots, places where there is free alkaline material on or near the surface, which would react chemically with oil-based primers. Acrylic latex primers are often used in this case, because they are less susceptible to alkali burns than oil-based products. Severe alkali problems require special sealers. These sealers must themselves be compatible with the paint that goes on top of them. It is best to talk to a professional about a complete coating system if you are dealing with difficult alkaline conditions.

Another special problem is posed by the rough, porous surface of masonry. Solve it with block filler latex primers and paints. These have enough build to make a solid surface on a raw cinder block wall in a single coat.

Visibly wet seeps on a masonry wall prevent every kind of primer and paint from sticking. However, if you have just a small amount of water vapor on masonry, latex primers and paints will last where oil-based products will not.

Oil-Based Masonry Primers

The same oil-based primers that are used on wood also serve well for masonry in good condition, provided that there is no moisture coming from behind the wall. Oil-based primers are more forgiving of a little dust or residual chalking than are latex primers.

Surface Conditioners

Occasionally, masonry surfaces seem to retain a layer of chalk dust no matter what you do to get rid of it. In this case, the problem is more than one of surface chalking; it calls for oil-based surface conditioners. These primers typically take up to seven days to cure. When the surface is so deteriorated that conditioners are needed, they must be applied in such a way as to ensure that they will work their way into the surface. Apply them with a brush or carefully with a roller. Surface conditioners should never be applied over peeling or flaking paint.

Metal Primers

Easily weathered metal requires primers with special chemical properties.

Iron and Steel Primers

Because they rust easily when exposed to water and moist air, iron and steel need extra protection. Unchecked, rust will eventually destroy them. The traditional primers for these metals were solvent based, and many contained red lead or other toxic compounds. Newer products contain few or no toxic ingredients. Many water-based products are coming to market that promise to perform the same functions as the traditional solvent-based ones.

Bright-Metal Primers

New metal, and old metal that has been completely cleaned of rust and shows a bright finish, must be primed. Use bright-metal primers. These will perform better than rusty-metal primers.

Rusty-Metal Primers

Old iron and steel that still shows rust should be primed with rusty-metal primers. In spite of the name, these products should not be applied over loose rust. Remove as much as you can with a reasonable effort. There will still be a layer of rust on the surface of the metal. These primers are meant to cover that final layer and to inhibit its further growth.

Rust Converters

Copper, brass, and silver form a surface layer of corrosion that protects them from further chemical reaction with the environment—a corrosion that prevents further corrosion. Rust converters help iron to do the same thing. These products are applied as a wash over the rust. They promote a chemical reaction that changes the rust into other, harmless, iron compounds that form a protective layer. Because they act only on the rust and do little to protect the unrusted metal, you must still prime the latter. Where rust is extensive they can be used as the only primer.

Galvanized Steel and Aluminum Primers

The traditional primers for aluminum and galvanized steel are zinc chromates, oil-based products that adhere very well and offer excellent protection. In some areas, zinc chromates are outlawed or restricted. Fortunately, there is an alternative, water-based metal primers. They are easy to clean up, have a short drying time, and can be applied to new metal without etching it first.

Primers for Various Construction Materials

This chart shows which primers are used to cover various types of construction material. Notice that some surfaces can be covered successfully with more than one type of primer. The chart helps you to distinguish between the possible and the preferred. Equally important, it shows which primers are unsuitable.

| | Construction Materials | | | | | |
Priming Materials	Sound Paint With Slight Residual Chalking	Sound, Clean, Absorbent Dry, Patching Materials	Bare Masonry	Bare Wood, Except Staining Woods[9]	Bare Staining Woods: Cedar, Redwood, etc.	Vinyl-Coated Siding
Latex exterior wood primer	Not recommended	Acceptable, but not best	Acceptable, but not best	Best	Not recommended	Acceptable, but not best[1]
Latex stucco conditioner	Not recommended	Acceptable, but not best	Best	Acceptable, but not best	Not recommended	Not recommended
Latex block filler	Not recommended	Not applicable	Applicable or best	Not recommended	Not recommended	Not recommended
Water-based masonry sealer	Not recommended	Not applicable	Best or not recommended[2]	Not recommended	Not recommended	Not recommended
Latex galvanized metal primer	Not applicable	Not applicable	Not applicable	Not applicable	Not applicable	Not recommended
Latex metal primer	Not applicable	Not applicable	Not applicable	Not applicable	Not applicable	Not recommended
Ordinary latex house paint	Not recommended	Acceptable, but not best	Acceptable, but not best	Acceptable, but not best	Not recommended	Best
Alkyd-modified latex house paint	Not recommended	Acceptable, but not best	Acceptable, but not best	Acceptable, but not best	Two coats may work	Acceptable, but not best
Oil-based exterior primer	Best	Acceptable, but not best	Acceptable, but not best	Acceptable, but not best	Best	Not recommended
"Long oil" oil-based exterior primer	Acceptable, but not best	Not recommended	Acceptable, but not best[4]	Not recommended	Acceptable, but not best	Not recommended
Zinc chromate green or yellow (oil based)	Not applicable	Not applicable	Not applicable	Not applicable	Not applicable	Not recommended
Oil-based rusty-metal primer	Not applicable	Not applicable	Not applicable	Not applicable	Not applicable	Not recommended
Rust converter	Not recommended	Not recommended	Not recommended	Not recommended	Not recommended	Not recommended
Pigmented shellac	Not recommended	Acceptable, but not best	Not recommended	Acceptable, but not best[6]	Acceptable, but not best[6]	Not recommended
Quick-drying oil-based primer	Acceptable, but not best	Acceptable, but not best	Not recommended	Acceptable, but not best[6]	Acceptable, but not best[6]	Not recommended

[1] Not necessary
[2] If to be painted
[3] OK if some bare metal
[4] Best if some chalking and no moisture
[5] Or OK, but not really recommended
[6] If small area
[7] Second rate
[8] If followed by full oil-based primer
[9] Spot-prime knots with shellac

Construction Materials

Baked Enamel Finishes, Properly Etched	Plastic	Bare Galvanized Steel	Bare Steel, Bright Metal	Bare Steel, Some Rust	Bare Steel, Extensive Tight Rust	Copper, Brass, or Bronze	Aluminum, Natural or Anodized	Asphalt Roofing Compounds
Not applicable	Acceptable, but not best[1]	Not recommended	Not recommended	Not recommended	Not recommended	Not recommended	Not recommended	Acceptable, but not best
Not applicable	Not recommended	Not recommended	Not recommended	Not recommended	Not recommended	Not recommended	Not recommended	Acceptable, but not best
Not applicable	Not recommended	Not recommended	Not recommended	Not recommended	Not recommended	Not recommended	Not recommended	Not recommended
Not recommended	Not recommended	Not recommended	Not recommended	Not recommended	Not recommended	Not recommended	Not recommended	Not recommended
Not applicable	Not recommended	Best	Not recommended	Not recommended	Not recommended	Not recommended	Acceptable, but not best	Not recommended
Not applicable[3]	Not recommended	Acceptable, but not best	Best	Acceptable, but not best	Acceptable, but not best	Not recommended	Best	Not recommended
Not recommended	Best	Not recommended	Not recommended	Not recommended	Not recommended	Not recommended	Acceptable, but not best	Best
Acceptable, but not best	Acceptable, but not best	Not recommended	Not recommended	Not recommended	Not recommended	Not recommended	Acceptable, but not best	Not recommended
Best	Not recommended	Not recommended	Acceptable, but not best[7]	Not recommended	Not recommended	Acceptable, but not best	Acceptable, but not best	Not recommended
Not recommended[5]	Not recommended	Not recommended	Acceptable, but not best[7]	Not recommended	Not recommended	Acceptable, but not best	Acceptable, but not best	Not recommended
Not recommended	Not recommended	Best	Not recommended	Not recommended	Not recommended	Best	Best	Not recommended
Not recommended	Not recommended	Not recommended	Acceptable, but not best	Best	Best	Not recommended	Acceptable, but not best	Not recommended
Not recommended	Not recommended	Not recommended	Not recommended	Acceptable, but not best[8]	Best	Not recommended	Not recommended	Not recommended
Not recommended	Not recommended	Not recommended	Not recommended	Not recommended	Not recommended	Not recommended	Not recommended	Not recommended
Acceptable, but not best[6]	Not recommended	Not recommended	Not recommended	Not recommended	Not recommended	Not recommended	Not recommended	Not recommended

PATCHING

Patching improves the appearance of a house and also helps to preserve it. Holes must be patched to keep moisture out. Areas where water, snow, and ice might collect should be patched to improve runoff. Although it can be difficult to make patched areas as sound as the original wood or masonry, this section explains how to do the best possible job.

Patching Uses

As you do your preparation, keep an eye out for certain kinds of imperfection. The most common surface problems are described on page 54. This list is not exhaustive, but it includes some of the things that will need patching.

All holes and cracks that would allow moisture to enter the structure must be patched before the finish coat is applied. In addition, you may want to make certain areas look good by filling imperfections.

Different patching materials are designed for different applications. There are several general factors to consider when choosing the right material for the job.

Shrinkage

Many patching materials shrink as they set. This means that if the surface of the patch is smooth and flat and even with the surrounding surface when it is applied, there will be a slight depression when the patch dries. The solution is either to apply enough extra material to compensate for the expected shrinkage or to make two applications.

Sandability

Some patching compounds can be sanded after they have set. Others set so hard that sanding is difficult. Still others can be shaped easily for only a short time after they are applied.

Curing Time

Drying time is important in planning the preparation and priming schedule. It is also a consideration in choosing the right material for the job.

Flexibility

When flexibility is essential, caulk and related compounds are the best answer (see page 74). Sometimes, of course, rigidity is required. In general, the patch should be as flexible or as rigid as it needs to be in order to move with the material to which it is attached.

Patching Materials

It is very important that the patch should adhere to the surface. Preparation of the surface is one factor in adhesion, but the type of material and the size and shape of the area to be patched are important, too. Check product labels for specific application and cleanup procedures.

Traditional Spackling Compound

Exterior spackling compounds are used to smooth out rough surfaces before painting. They come in the form of a dry powder to be mixed in water or of a ready-mixed paste. The paste is somewhat easier to use. Spackling compounds set by drying rather than by a chemical reaction. The thicker you apply them, the longer they will take to dry. If the compound is applied too thick, it will dry like mud and crack. The best spackling compounds shrink very little as they dry.

Spackling compound is appropriate for filling nail holes, for filling shallow gouges and irregularities, and for smoothing out rough surfaces. It is not suitable for filling large holes, because it is not particularly strong. Neither should it be used for filling gouges in structural elements, such as porches or steps.

Even so-called exterior compounds must be well protected from the weather by primer and one or more finish coats. They are very absorbent, and the primer is necessary to prevent flashing.

The main advantages of spackling compound are that it is easy to sand smooth and that it dries relatively fast. A thin coat used to hide the chips flaked off a single coat of paint may dry in an hour or less. A thicker coat may take a day to dry completely. If it takes more than a day of good weather to dry, the application is too thick, or it is being used in an inappropriate location. If the hole to be filled is more than 1 inch across and deeper than ¼ inch or so, it is better to make two thin applications than one thick one. The total drying time will be shorter, because the dried surface of a deep patch inhibits the drying of the core.

Remember that spackling compound shrinks as it dries. A slight overfilling is all that is required to make a single application (and a single sanding) serve for most patches.

Lightweight Spackling

A relatively new product, lightweight spackling compound, is gaining wide acceptance. Its main feature is that a large amount of air is trapped in the structure of the material, making it phenomenally light. Its greatest advantage as far as many painters are concerned is that it can be painted over immediately, while it is still soft, with latex products, and it will still dry. This makes it possible to patch, smooth, and prime all in one step. Lightweight spackling compound is slightly better than traditional spackling compound for filling large voids; however, it is not as good for filling wide, shallow imperfections. Nor does it sand as smooth as traditional products. It dries in about the same amount of time.

Linseed Oil Putty

The traditional material for filling holes and cracks in wood is putty. Putty is a mixture of a drying oil, such as linseed or soybean; fillers; and extenders. It dries very slowly; a skin will form on its surface in a day or so, and it will continue to dry over a period of weeks or months depending on the thickness of the application.

Once the skin has formed, it can be painted. If painted before then, the oil in the putty may migrate through the paint to the surface of the finish coat and leave spots.

Any surface to be patched with putty should be primed first. This prevents the putty from drying out too quickly.

The chief advantage of putty is that it can be applied flush with the surface; it doesn't shrink and it doesn't need sanding. The slow drying time can be a disadvantage or an advantage depending on the schedule. It is quite safe to leave putty patches exposed from one weekend to the next without priming over them.

Cement Products

Large cracks in mortar, cement, or stucco are patched with various kinds of cement. All of these products are powders that bond together when mixed with the correct amount of water. The longer they remain damp, the stronger they will be when they finally set.

Stucco Patch

Stucco is cement that has enough body to allow it to be built up on a vertical surface. Ready-mixed stucco patch is available from various manufacturers.

Stucco patch must be mixed with the right amount of water to bond properly. Follow the directions on the package. When you make only a small amount, aim for a light mixture that is capable of being piled up and holding its shape. It should not be fluid at all.

Stucco patch is neither glue nor mortar. It does not perform well in thin layers, either on the surface of the wall or in a thin crack. On the other hand,

Patching preserves the integrity of the house by preventing water from entering the structure and causing damage. Wood near areas where water runs off from the roof, such as on the deck on this stained house, are especially vulnerable. Patch and sand problem surfaces before staining.

Patching a Stucco Wall

1. Partially fill hole, using applicator to score surface so next coat can lock onto it

Rough surface

2. Apply finish coat smooth and flat leaving a little excess material

Smooth surface

Trowel

Patch even with surrounding stucco

Rag

3. Smooth off excess material

it will sag if it is laid on too thick, especially if there is no framework to support it. When a house is coated with stucco, a frame of chicken wire is strung on nails over the vapor barrier. Spacers on the nails hold the wire a little way out from the wall. The first, or scratch, coat of stucco is applied to the framework. The surface of this coat is scored deeply before it sets, to provide a series of grooves into which the next coat of stucco locks.

If you have a fairly large area to patch (say 1 or 2 square feet) and it is deeper than an inch or so, you may need to approximate this technique. Apply the stucco patch in two coats and score the first one to hold the second one in place.

Be sure to clean loose material, dirt, and dust out of the area to be patched. Then dampen it. This prevents the water in the stucco patch from leaching into the surrounding stucco before it has a chance to cure.

When you apply the final coat of stucco, mound it up and spread it over the adjoining areas. When it begins to set, but before it has set completely, carve off the excess and wipe down the area with a rag and a bucket of water. Be careful; the water will weaken the top layer of stucco. When the stucco has set firmly and the top is dry, brush off this weakened layer. You will be left with a firm, sound surface.

Don't apply stucco patch in the direct afternoon sun. If stucco dries before it sets properly, it will crumble. It will also crumble if the proportions of the mixture were wrong. Follow the manufacturer's directions to the letter.

Mortar

A mixture of cement, lime, and sand, mortar is used to bind masonry together. Sometimes other chemicals are added to improve its performance. Mortar is available ready mixed in small quantities.

If the area to be repaired is small, it may be worthwhile to do the job yourself. If much of the mortar is in bad repair, consider having the bricks or stone repointed by a professional. This is a matter not just of aesthetics but of structural soundness. In general, the only time that some, but not all, of the joints will need repair will be when the damage is due to settling of the foundation. This produces cracks even in sound mortar. If it is a case of general deterioration, you have a bigger problem on your hands than a 25-pound sack of mortar can solve.

To patch an area of mortar, remove all the loose material in the joints between the bricks, blocks, or stone. Wet the area down with water. The mortar should not dry out before it has a chance to set. Mix the mortar patch according to the directions on the package. A pointing trowel is useful for pushing the mortar into the joints between the bricks and for smoothing out or raking off the excess mortar. Use a dry or slightly damp rag to remove any smears.

A week or so after you have applied the mortar, it will be set sufficiently to enable you to clean up the last stains and smears. Remove dried cement and cement products from masonry surfaces with a dilute solution of muriatic (hydrochloric) acid. The approximate proportions are 10 parts of water to 1 part of acid. Be extremely careful. Acid can burn skin and eyes. Follow all the precautions on the label. The rule for mixing acid and water is: Acid to Water = All's Well, Water to Acid = Watch your Assets! This is one rule that is important to get right.

Wash down the stained areas with a stiff brush and the dilute acid. The acid will do most of the work by attacking the lime and cement that hold the mortar together. This is why it is important to wait until the mortar is well cured before you clean up. If you were to do it sooner, the acid would migrate right through the unset mortar, breaking it down as it went. If you wait, it will attack only the top $1/16$ inch of material, leaving the rest untouched.

When you have finished etching off the stains, wash down the entire work surface (and the area below it) with plenty of water.

Resin Products

Epoxy and urethane patching materials have several advantages over other products. They are particularly useful for filling deep imperfections in wood, which are difficult to patch in any other way.

Resin Fillers

These are what body shops use to build out dents in cars. Known by brand names such as Bondo, they consist of a filler and a hardener. These must be mixed in the proportions specified on the label. The chemical reaction that results causes the material to set up quickly. Working time is indicated on the container. (This is the amount of time it takes for the material to begin to set, at which point it can no longer be shaped easily.)

While the material is workable, it is a sticky paste. It can be pushed into holes and smoothed off with a putty knife or spatula. For a short time it can be carved. When it sets hard, it can be shaped only by sanding, preferably with an electric sander.

A typical residential use for resin fillers is to fill a long crack in a pillar holding up a porch. Long cracks occur when the wood dries, especially in large pieces, such as 4 by 4 beams. They can be fairly wide and deep. Because they move with changes in the weather (swelling and shrinking as the wood absorbs moisture and dries out), spackling compound and putty can work their way out. Resin fillers hang on a little better. They will also set uniformly regardless of the depth of the patch.

Wood Hardeners

Resin products are also used to repair dry rot and wet rot. All the old rot should be removed, or killed with a biocide designed for that purpose, before the hole is filled. If this is not done, the rot may continue to grow behind the patch.

In the past rot damage was difficult to repair. Even if the rot itself was stopped, the remaining damaged wood was usually too soft to hold the patch. Today you can solve this problem with chemical wood hardeners. These are very thin volatile compounds that penetrate the damaged wood fibers, destroying any rot and driving any water ahead of them. When they have soaked into the wood, they set hard in a few hours, forming a sound surface that will hold a patch. The key to successful repair is to remove as much loose material as possible before you use the hardener.

Apply wood hardeners with a disposable bristle brush. Keep applying until the damaged wood has soaked up as much as it will hold. These products are very thin and watery. It is impossible to keep them from dripping, so protect the surfaces below the work area.

Urethane Foam

Here is another, very different, resin product. Urethane foam was originally designed as insulation to be injected into walls. Foam comes out of a nozzle in a spray can, expanding instantly to many times its original volume. When it stops expanding, it starts to harden; within a short time it is set. At this point it has the structure of foam rubber and the weight and hardness of polystyrene. It can be sawed or cut with a knife. Unfortunately, the application of foam is difficult to control. Once out of the can, it just expands in every available direction to the limit of its ability. On the other hand, that is why foam can be used to patch holes that have nothing behind them. An example would be a hole in a concrete block.

Follow the directions on the container. Make sure that the first bit of foam you apply is touching some surface inside the hole. It must touch something to get an initial grip; it cannot simply be squirted into thin air. Two applications may be required to patch a particularly difficult area.

When the foam has set, carve or sand off the excess. Smooth the surface of the patch by applying a firm-textured product, such as spackling compound or resin filler.

Using Patching Materials

Most patching materials are pastes of one kind or another. Though each has its own characteristics, they are all applied in much the same way.

Drop and mask around the area to be patched (see page 24) and follow access safety procedures (see page 20).

The object of patching is to apply the material in such a way as to fill the space completely while keeping the top of the patch as smooth and as flush with the surrounding area as possible. The easiest way to do this is to apply the material with a putty knife or, for large areas, with a broad knife. Pick up some of the patching material and carry it on the knife to the hole. Push it in, making sure that all parts of the hole are completely filled. Smooth the patch with a single stroke of the knife, if possible. This will be easier if the knife is wide enough that, as you drag it along, its outside edges rest on a hard, flat surface.

Properties of Patching Materials

This chart shows the properties of various patching materials discussed in this chapter. Knowing the properties of the materials helps you to know how to apply them and in what circumstances to use them. Where smoothness is the goal, use materials that can be sanded whenever possible. Where flexibility is an issue, that property takes precedence.

	Shrinkage	Sandability	Curing Time	Flexibility	Can be Used in Thick Layers?	Need to Prime Behind?	Need to Prime Over?
General Patching Materials							
Spackling compounds, traditional	20%	Easy	Moderate to fast	None	Very slow drying	Helps	Yes
Spackling compounds, lightweight	10%	Very easy	Fast	None	Slow drying	Helps	Yes
Linseed oil putty	5%	None	Very slow	High for 1st yr. or so, then low	Adequate	Must	No
Stucco patch	1%	None	Moderate	None	Must be	Must not	W/acrylic if topcoat is oil based
Mortar	1%	None	Moderate	None	Adequate	Must not	W/acrylic if topcoat is oil based
Resin fillers	1%	Moderate	Moderate to fast	Low	Good	No need	No
Wood hardeners	N/A	Moderate	Moderate	Low	N/A	Must not	N/A
Urethane foam	Expands	Easy	Fast	Low	Good	No need	No
Caulking Materials							
Latex, white or colored	30%	None	Moderate	High	N/A	Helps	No
Latex with silicone, white	30%	None	Moderate	High	N/A	Helps	No
Latex with silicone, clear	30%	None	Moderate	High	N/A	Helps	No
Elastomeric terpolymer, gun grade	20%	None	Moderate	Very high	N/A	Helps	No
Butyl rubber	20%	None	Moderate	Very high	N/A	No need, but helps	No
Pure silicone	20%	None	Moderate	Very high	N/A	No need, but helps	Yes
Clear solvent based, not silicone	20%	None	Moderate	Very high	N/A	No need, but helps	No
Flexible Patching Materials							
Acrylic latex, knife grade	35%	None	Moderate to fast	High	N/A	Should	No
Elastomeric terpolymer, knife grade	25%	None	Moderate to fast	Very high	N/A	Should	No
Elastomeric terpolymer, brush grade	40%	None	Fast	Very high	N/A	Must	No
Sandable semiflexible materals	20%	Moderate	Moderate	Moderate	Very slow drying	No need	Yes

SEALING WINDOWPANES

Most windowpanes are sealed against the weather with a high-grade putty known as glazing compound. Like all putties, eventually the compound will weather and crack. This allows moisture to enter behind it and push it away from the sash and the glass. If the compound is not repaired, the water will attack the sash or the muntins.

Removing Old Compound

As you do the preparation, check the glazing compound on each window. Pry out any loose compound with a stiff putty knife. Scrape any loose material, such as alligatored paint, from the surface of the compound. Sand or scrape any bare sash or muntins back to a clean surface.

To remove firmly attached old glazing compound, soften it with a heat gun. (If you try to remove it by force, you are likely to break the window.) Move along slowly, keeping the gun moving back and forth, heating and scraping as you go. Be careful not to scorch the wood.

Before you apply new compound, apply quick-drying primer to bare wood sashes and muntins.

Applying New Compound

Use glazing compound and a specially shaped putty knife to seal a window.

Cold glazing compound is too stiff to be worked, and it will not adhere to the window. Use it when it is warm enough to stick, but not so warm that it won't hold its shape. Cool it down by setting it in a cool place. Warm it up by kneading it like clay.

To fill shallow cracks in otherwise sound glazing compound, scrape the loose material and apply a thin coat of new compound. Dampen a rag with paint thinner, wrap it around your finger, and smooth off the surface. (You can't do this if the compound is deep. It will make it very uneven.) When the glazing compound dries enough to form a skin, it can be painted.

To seal an entire window, start with a clean, primed sash. Make sure that the glazing compound is at the right consistency. Take a lump large enough to fill one complete run of sash. Push it into place with the knife, overfilling slightly. Don't worry about getting it smooth. Just make sure that there is enough compound all the way along one side of the window to fill the space completely, with no gaps and no air behind the glazing compound.

Now press the compound firmly into place, both against the glass and against the sash. This is easiest to do with two hands, one supplying pressure toward the glass and the other toward the sash. Hold the edge of the knife at a shallow angle. If you rake it along perpendicular to the compound (as if it were a brush) you will pull the compound out or rough it up. The surface should be smooth, and the gap should be filled between the face of the sash and a point on the window just high enough to cover the wood on the inside. The back of the glazing compound should not be visible when you look out the window from inside the house.

Now put the knife at one end of this first run of compound. Rest the blade on the sash. Put one corner of the blade at the point on the window where you want the surface of the finished compound to be. Hold the handle of the knife as low to the sash as possible. Draw the knife along this run, pushing the compound firmly into place and smoothing its surface in one continuous motion. When you get to the end of the run, cut off the excess at the corner.

Smears of oil on the glass can be wiped off more easily if they are left to dry for a day. Solid pieces of compound are easier to remove when they are still soft.

Repeat this process for each side of the window. Work fairly quickly in cool weather. Once the material is in the sash, it starts to cool. If it cools too much before it is smoothed down, it will pull out when you drag the knife along it. The only solution then is to pull the compound out, warm it up in your hands, and start over.

Allow the surface of the compound to form a skin before you paint it. This can take several days, depending on drying conditions. If glazing compound is painted before it has dried sufficiently, the paint will dry faster than the compound, and it will alligator.

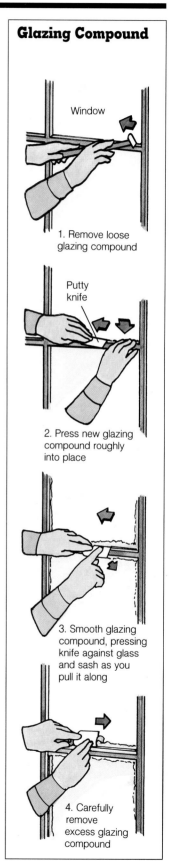

Glazing Compound

1. Remove loose glazing compound

Window

Putty knife

2. Press new glazing compound roughly into place

3. Smooth glazing compound, pressing knife against glass and sash as you pull it along

4. Carefully remove excess glazing compound

SING CAULK AND FLEXIBLE PATCHING MATERIALS

Gaps in surfaces that move a lot require a flexible patch. Use caulk to seal gaps between different types of building materials. The different rates of expansion and contraction will quickly break out a rigid patch. Use flexible patching materials for a large area covered with a network of cracks.

Caulking Uses

When you inspect the house, look for places in need of caulking. These will include any joint between two different materials, such as wood and masonry, wood and metal, and plastic and metal. They will also include joints between two pieces of wood in a window frame or a doorframe. The bottom and top edges of overlapped pieces of siding do not need to be caulked, but caulk any vertical joints, as well as any cracks in a single board.

Latex caulk can be used as a last-minute patch for nail holes and small gaps that you discover when you apply a latex finish coat. You can paint directly over the wet caulk. Because the materials are similar and the latex paint can breathe, the caulk will set anyway.

Caulking Materials

Caulks can be divided into water-based emulsion types—acrylic latex and some silicones—and solvent-based types—other silicones and butyl rubber. The old oil-based caulks have been abandoned, for the most part, because they tended to harden too much as

they dried, making them less flexible than current versions.

Water-Based Types

Factors to consider when choosing which type of caulk to use are adhesion, color (or lack thereof), and durability.

Acrylic Latex

These durable caulks are easily cleaned up with water. They hold paint, particularly latex paint, very well, and they come in various grades, the more durable ones being a bit more expensive. The products that contain the most liquid shrink the most; lay down the bead of caulk accordingly. Acrylic latex caulk comes in a limited range of colors. Use the one that comes closest to matching the paint color, which makes it a little easier to cover in one coat.

Acrylic latex caulk is sometimes combined with silicone to form a more durable product. Acrylic/silicone caulks are available in tints and in clear formulations. Use the latter where the caulk must be applied

over the finish coat, rather than the other way around.

Elastomeric Terpolymers

Sealants made of elastomeric terpolymer are also available in caulking-gun grades for patching cracks in masonry that is to be painted. They are very tough and flexible, and they can be cleaned up with water. They are considerably more expensive than acrylic latex caulks, but they remain flexible for a much longer time.

Silicones

Caulks made of silicone are very resistant to heat, water, and corrosion. Some silicones clean up with water, others with solvents. Check the label on the product. Silicone adheres well to sound porous surfaces. Pure silicone is expensive, but it is one of the best clear caulks. Its major drawback is that it is too smooth to accept paint well. The paint will crawl off the surface of the silicone rather than forming an even film. If this product has been used to caulk parts of the house, the best solution is to pull off as much as possible and prime whatever remains with a solvent-based primer. Pure silicone has a low resistance to solvents. Silicone is a good choice for use over transparent stains.

Use caulk to fill gaps between different building materials, such as the brick and the horizontal board siding on this ranch house, and around roof vents. Remember that vents should be painted to match other metal features.

Using a Caulking Gun

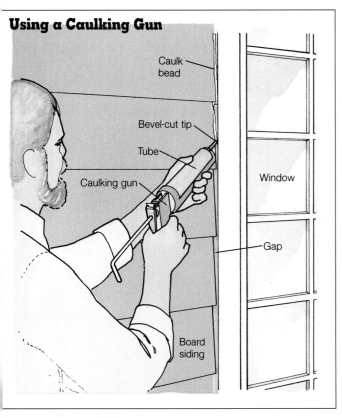

Caulk bead

Bevel-cut tip

Tube

Caulking gun

Window

Gap

Board siding

Solvent-Based Types

Clear solvent-based caulking compounds are more difficult to use than water-based products. Some of them are stickier than rubber cement. However, if the correct solvent is used, they can be applied smoothly. Their advantages are their excellent adhesion, durability, ability to remain clearer longer than water-based ones, and, best of all, the ease with which they accept paint.

Flexible Patching Materials

Occasionally, you may need to cover a large area with a flexible patch. An example might be a section of stucco that is crisscrossed with many hairline cracks. Rather than patching

each crack individually, apply a coat of flexible waterproof patch to the whole area. Elastomeric terpolymer sealants are ideal for this job. They are essentially the same as the caulking compounds, but they are available in different viscosities for application by trowel or brush and roller. Make sure that the surface to be covered is clean, sound, and dry. These sealants are truly waterproof.

Using Caulk

Caulk must remain firmly attached to both sides of the gap it is intended to fill. If either side is covered with a layer of surface dirt or chalking paint, for example, the caulk will pull

away from that side, breaking the seal. This is why you should prime before you caulk.

All the most commonly used caulks and flexible patches shrink as they cure. When this happens, holes may open up in the bead of caulk. Sometimes a second application of caulk will solve this problem. If the crack is too wide, however, you must fill it with something else before you apply new caulk.

In the days of wooden ships, the seams between the boards were caulked by pounding treated jute fibers, called oakum, into the gap with a mallet. The caulker came behind with a can full of boiling tar or pitch and poured a thin stream onto the fibers to seal them. There is no need for you to look around for oakum, however. Foam rubber filler rope comes in several different diameters and is soft enough to be pushed into place with a putty knife. No mallets needed.

Caulk is usually sold in tubes intended to be used in a caulking gun. Cut the tip of the tube to make the right-sized opening for the job at hand: small for a thin bead, wide for a thick one. It is better to have the opening too small than too large. Make sure to bevel the cut. This will make it easier to apply a smooth bead. If there is a seal inside the tube at the base of the tip, puncture it with a nail or a piece of wire. Pull the plunger all the way back and place the tube in the gun. Push the plunger until it snugs up to the diaphragm at the back of the tube. Squeeze the trigger until the caulk begins to flow out; then stop the flow.

Some guns are designed so that the flow stops as soon as the pressure on the trigger is released. Others have a button to push to relieve the pressure, and in still others you turn the shaft of the plunger.

For smoothing, wet a clean rag with the correct solvent for the material you are using: water for latex and some silicone caulks; appropriate chemical solvents for solvent-based and other silicone caulks. Caulk is impossible to shape once it has cured, so be prepared to smooth as you go.

Put the tip of the gun at one end of the crack and squeeze the trigger slowly as you move the gun along it. Push or pull, whichever is easier. Put enough caulk into the crack to touch both sides of the gap and fill it up to just above the surface.

When you have laid a bead of the right size along the whole crack (or as far as you can reach from one position), wrap your finger in the rag and run it along the caulk to smooth it out. If you have not put down enough, gaps will appear. If you have put down too much, you will pick it up. Remember that caulk shrinks as it cures. Don't be so stingy with it that you have to go back and apply a second coat where it might not have been necessary otherwise. In addition to making the job look neater, this smoothing process helps to spread the caulk along the area immediately next to the crack. This gives it a much wider surface to hang onto, which in turn helps it to withstand the expansion and contraction of the gap.

PAINTING AND STAINING

A wide variety of materials is available for beautifying a house and protecting it from the elements. They range from simple clear oil finishes through stains, paints, and elastomeric sealants. What is right for your house depends partly on the materials from which it is constructed and greatly on the effect you want to achieve. This chapter describes the various products and explains how to apply them. It includes tips for painting special effects and for adding individualized finishing touches. It also discusses cleanup, storage, and disposal.

Choosing the correct house paint involves more than merely picking a color. Choose the paint that best suits the structure to ensure that the job will last. An older wood house, such as this Queen Anne Victorian, should be painted with a low-sheen finish coat, which helps camouflage surface imperfections.

CHOOSING THE RIGHT MATERIALS

Paint, stain, varnish, oil finishes, and water-proofing materials are all composed of chemicals that remain liquid in the can and on the brush but that dry when exposed to air. This section discusses the composition of paint in detail. The other products are described by comparing them to paint.

Composition of Paint

Three basic classes of media are important in house painting. These are oil-based paint, in which the vehicle is a drying oil, such as linseed or soy; latex paint, in which the vehicle is a water-based emulsion; and solvent products, including varnishes and certain specialty finishes. All three work in the same general way.

The first paints were nothing more than pigments mixed with some medium, such as milk, wax, or water and lime. Although the technology has changed, the basic principle remains the same. There must be some way of getting the pigment onto the wall in a smooth, even coat and some mechanism to keep it there.

Basically, modern paint consists of a vehicle, thinning agents, and pigments. It also contains fillers, extenders, and other additives.

Vehicle

The vehicle, also called the medium or binder, is the mechanism that allows the mixture to remain liquid in the can and on the brush or roller and then allows it to set once on the wall so that the pigment holds firmly in place.

Once paint is exposed to air, it loses its volatile component and the vehicle gradually sets into a solid coat. The properties of this coat depend on the vehicle. In the case of oil-based paints and varnishes, the coat is hard and impermeable to air and moisture. In the case of most latex paints, the coat is less hard and is permeable to small amounts of water vapor.

Thinning Agent

To make paint easier to spread and to use, it is thinned with an agent that will evaporate once the paint is applied. In the case of latex paints, this is water. In the case of oil-based paints, it is mineral spirits or paint thinner. Some specialty products are thinned with more powerful solvents, such as acetone and alcohol.

Pigment

The coloring agents in paint are called pigments. They include a wide variety of chemicals. Some of these, sienna and umber, for example, are naturally occurring compounds. Many more are chemically engineered. The most important white pigment is titanium oxide. Zinc oxide is also used as a white pigment and to improve brushing characteristics.

Paint Composition

Typical Paint
- Solvent
- Fillers and extenders
- Additives
- Vehicle
- Pigment

High-Quality Paint
- Solvent
- Vehicle
- Pigment
- Fillers and extenders
- Additives

Different surfaces require different painting techniques. This multiple color design should be executed with a roller.

How to Thin Paint and Why

Most paints are the right consistency when you buy them. They don't need thinning. For application with a brush or roller, you will need to add thinning agent only when hot weather or long exposure to air has evaporated part of the agent that was originally present in the paint.

The thinning agent for oil-based paint is mineral spirits, usually called paint thinner. Because paint thinner is more volatile than water, oil-based paint needs thinning more often than latex. Latex usually requires thinning only on a very hot, dry day. In either case, be judicious in the use of thinning agents. They are easy to add but impossible to take out. If you add too much water to latex paint, it will no longer form an even coat. Beyond a certain point it won't even be paint anymore. That point is reached more quickly adding water to latex than it is adding thinner to oil-based paint.

The object of thinning paint is to make it easier to use effectively. If the paint is too thick, it will be difficult to brush out; it will build up too thick a coat when used with a roller; and it will sag. If it is too thin, however, it will not spread evenly or cover well, and it will drip and run excessively.

Thinning agents can be used to combat less-than-ideal weather conditions (see page 11). If you apply latex paint on the sunny side of the house on a warm day, it will set up quickly, becoming tacky almost as soon as it hits the building. If you mist the side of the building with water from the garden hose—please note: It says mist, not soak—this will cool the building and leave a very small amount of water on the surface. The building should be just cool to the touch; it should not feel wet, if you want the paint job to remain intact.

When the weather is too cool to use latex, you can still use oil paint. You should thin it a bit more than usual because it tends to thicken at lower temperatures. However, cool weather is often wet weather. Remember that oil-based paint must not be used on a damp surface.

Adding thinning agents changes drying times slightly. This can lead to minor variations in gloss level or even, in a few cases, in color. This is most important in spray applications, where a large part of the house will be covered with material that has been thinned. It is always good policy to thin as much paint as you need to complete one whole section (say, one side of the house) all at once. In this way, you can minimize any variations. Save a bit of the thinned paint for touch-ups.

Note: For more than two centuries lead oxides were the single most important class of pigments in house paint. Because of their toxicity, the use of lead compounds in paint has been outlawed in the United States. The use of white lead, by far the most common, was made illegal in 1969. Use of the remaining lead compounds, primarily in driers and in red lead pigment for rust-inhibitive primers, was discontinued in 1978. The few products still containing lead are not available to the general public. Their use is restricted to industrial applications where human contact is not an issue.

Many paints contain extenders or fillers, such as silica or chalk. These materials are technically classed as pigments, but they are not powerful coloring agents. They are added to improve the thickness of the dried paint; to improve coverage or opacity; to change the brushing characteristics of the product; and to flat out, or reduce the sheen of, the finish. In the least expensive paints, these extenders are actually substituted for titanium oxides and other more powerful white pigments.

Additives

In addition to the basic ingredients, modern paints contain many additives. Oil-based paints need chemicals called driers to speed the setting process. Latex paints are sensitive to freezing and thawing and typically have antifreeze compounds added to them. Latex and other emulsion paints also contain chemicals that help to keep the resins suspended in the water. Antimildew ingredients are usually added to both oil and latex paints. This is most important in extending the shelf life of latex. Paint may also contain small amounts of various other chemicals that make it easier to apply, allow it to dry to a more even sheen, and improve its durability.

Spurred on by stiffer pollution control laws and consumer demand, latex paint technology is improving steadily. Many modern latex paints contain alkyd resins. (Alkyds are the main vehicle in a large class of oil-based paints.) By suspending these resins in the latex paint, manufacturers can gain some of the advantages of oil-based paint while keeping most of the advantages of latex.

Properties of Paint

In comparing one paint with another, it is useful to have a vocabulary to describe their most important properties. The painting trade has its own terms for things, but they are simple and easy to remember.

Opacity

This word describes how well new paint covers the existing color. Opacity is a function of the evenness with which the paint is applied and the type and amount of pigment in the paint. (The difference between the new and old color is a factor too, of course.)

White and black tend to cover well. Earth colors (sienna and umber) cover fairly well. Typical paint formulas have some white pigment in them. The purer the color desired, the less white and black there will be in the mixture.

Ironically, the least expensive white paints often cover the best. This is because they contain large amounts of chalk. The ultimate example is whitewash, a paste made of lime. It covers very well, but it is subject to chalking, and it must be reapplied once a year.

Viscosity and Spreadability

Viscosity is the thickness of liquid paint. Spreadability is just what it sounds like. Most paints are sold with a viscosity for spreading with brush or roller. Some primers may require thinning first; use the thinner specified on the label. Most paints must be thinned slightly for use in a sprayer.

Build

The thickness of the dried paint is its build. Oil-based paints tend to have less build than latex paints. However, a given oil-based paint will have slightly less build if it is thinned with mineral spirits than if it is not thinned.

The thickness of paint films is measured in thousandths of an inch, so it may be hard to believe that build is significant, but sometimes it is. The window that closes easily and snugly when the wood is bare may stick or be hard to close once it is primed and painted. A few mils' thickness of paint can make a difference.

Hold-Out

The ability to keep stains from coming through the paint up to the surface is called hold-out. Oil-based paints and varnishes have good hold-out. Latex paints are permeable to small amounts of water vapor. This is an advantage in many respects, but it reduces their ability to hold out water-soluble stains. If you are using latex paint and think staining will be a problem, consider priming the area first with an oil-based product.

Drying Time

All paint products go from a liquid state through various stages of drying to a full cure. The first stage is when the paint is still wet to the touch, but it is beginning to set up and has become tacky. At this point it begins to pull—a bit like taffy—when spread with a brush. Instead of spreading out smoothly, it grabs, and the brush marks will not flatten out. Do not attempt to touch up paint when it is in this state. You will only make matters worse. If you brush into a tacky area by mistake, and you want the job to look perfect, the only thing to do is to wait until it has dried completely, sand out the offending brush marks, and repaint. This is a lot of work, so consider carefully whether it is necessary.

The next stage of drying is called dry to the touch or surface dry. Some labels specify that the product dries dust free in a certain time. This means that after that time the product will no longer be so sticky that dust in the air is trapped on its surface. However, the paint is not yet fully cured.

After dry to the touch comes dry enough to recoat. The label will distinguish between these two stages. Many oil-based paints are dry to the touch in 2 or 3 hours but must dry for 6 or 8 or even 24 hours before they can be recoated.

Latex finish coats are generally ready for recoating sooner than oil-based finish coats. However, the same cautions apply to both. If you paint over a fresh coat of paint or varnish too soon, the water or solvents in the second coat may soften the first coat enough to make it tacky again. If you apply a layer of quick-drying product over a layer of slow-drying product that is not yet set, the top layer may harden and shrink independently of the bottom one. This causes alligatoring and crazing.

A surface that is dry enough to recoat has not yet reached full cure. A week after you apply it, the paint will still be getting harder. This is important for two reasons. First, particularly with latex paints, resistance to abrasion is not as high as it will be when the paint is fully cured. Decks, thresholds, doors, and windows should be treated gently for the first few days. Second,

Metal surfaces, such as this intricate wrought-iron security gate, must be painted with a rust-inhibitive product.

e sheen of some paints will ange gradually as they cure. light variations in the sheen f low-gloss paints caused by neven curing of the vehicle hould disappear over a period f several months. When all of ne paint is fully cured, it will ll have the same sheen.

Weather affects drying time. he drying times given by anufacturers are for normal onditions, which are 70° F, noderate humidity, light or no reeze, and no direct sunlight. very variation from this hypo- netical norm will change the rying time to some extent. Ieat, airflow, and low humid- y promote rapid drying. High umidity, lack of airflow, and w temperatures retard it. In act, latex paints will simply top curing when the tempera- ure drops below about 45° F.

evels of Gloss

Gloss, or sheen, is the degree to vhich a painted surface reflects ght. Most paint media natu- ally dry to a glossy surface. To reate flat, or matte, finishes nd other low-gloss effects, nanufacturers must add sili- ates and other ingredients.)ifferent manufacturers use dif- erent names to describe the evel of gloss in their products. A typical series is: high gloss, emigloss, satin finish, eggshell, ow lustre, and matte finish.

High-gloss paints look wet, ll glistening and shiny. Semi- loss paints are also shiny and mooth looking, but they don't nave the wet look of high-gloss aints. Semigloss is the most ommon finish for exterior trim.

Satin finish, eggshell, and low lustre are all variations within a midrange of gloss and vary from one manufacturer to another. Their sheen is most obvious when seen at the sur- face from a low angle—stand- ing at one corner of the house and looking along the wall, for example. A truly matte, or flat, finish looks like a piece of un- glazed tile or chalk. It breaks up the light completely and has no sheen at any angle. True mattes are difficult to find in unmodified latex house paints. In order to achieve durability, manufacturers limit the amount of flatting agent they put in their best-quality exte- rior paints.

Time and weather will usu- ally reduce the gloss level of any exterior product to some extent. Solid-body latex stains provide the flattest flat in exte- rior latex products.

Choosing levels of gloss is first and foremost an aesthetic decision. Higher glosses tend to show surface imperfections more and therefore require careful surface preparation. On the functional side, the gloss level indicates how smooth the surface of the paint film is. High-gloss and semigloss paints are less apt than flats to hold dirt and dust. To deal with this problem, traditional flat house paints are made to chalk (see page 54). That is, they wash themselves by losing their top layer at a controlled rate.

Note: High-gloss and semi- gloss surfaces have no tooth— no roughness to hold the next coat of paint. If you want to recoat an area painted with high gloss or semigloss, break up the surface a bit with sand- paper first.

The Nature of the Surface

The nature of the surface is important in respect to choos- ing paint. Glossy finishes show the unevenness of the surface much more than flat or low lustre finishes. If you are not prepared to take old, previ- ously painted trim back to a smooth surface, you should consider using a lower sheen finish material. Rough or heavily textured surfaces such as masonry and shingles are typically finished in low sheen materials for the same reason.

Penetrating clear wood seal- ers can only be used over new wood or wood that has been treated with the same type sealer before.

Semitransparent stains can be used only over new wood or wood that has been stained in the same color. (Using a differ- ent color of semitransparent stain is physically possible, but it would give very doubtful re- sults.) If you have new wood to treat or have areas of the house where these materials were used in the past, then these finishes are among your op- tions. Their chief advantages are that they require less prepa- ration and that they allow the color variations in the wood to show through.

Porches, decks, steps, and walkways should be painted with porch and deck enamel, which is much tougher than ordinary paint. However, it comes in a limited range of colors. Take these limitations into account when choosing a color scheme.

Metal railings and ornamen- tal ironwork should be coated with rust-inhibitive paints.

Latex and Oil-Based Paints

The first decision in choosing paint is whether to pick an oil- based or a latex product. The principle advantages of latex paints are their low odor, easy cleanup (using water rather than thinners), faster drying time and time to recoat, supe- rior build, and permeability to small amounts of water vapor. In addition, latex paints are less sensitive to alkali in the sur- face. This can be important if you are painting over cement or plaster.

Oil-based paints generally take longer to dry to the touch and to recoat, but they dry harder than latex, and once set they are impermeable. This gives them much better hold- out than latex paints and makes them more resistant to abra- sion. Oil-based paints have less build than latex paints, and so they go a little farther, covering a slightly larger area per gallon. Oil-based paints will bond with a surface that is slightly chalked.

In an effort to get the best of both worlds, many paint man- ufacturers are now making la- tex house paints that contain modified alkyd resins. These alkyd-modified latex paints are less sensitive to chalking sur- faces, are a bit more resistant to abrasion, and generally get a better grip on the surface than traditional latex formulations. They are not quite as perme- able to water vapor as unmodi- fied latex. They still breathe, however, and will allow some vapor to pass through. Alkyd- modified latex is also more trouble to clean up. Brushes must be washed in water and then rinsed in paint thinner.

Specialty Paints

Certain surfaces or materials require not only special primers but also special finish coats. These finishing materials are applied in the same way as any other paint of the same base, and cleanup is the same.

Rust-Inhibitive Paints

One class of paint gives extra protection against rust. If the iron or steel is properly prepared and primed, it is not necessary to use these products, but they will protect it better than standard house paint. Rust-inhibitive paints are available in latex and oil-based formulations. They may not be available in all colors, a point to keep in mind when designing the color scheme.

Porch and Deck Paints

Porches, decks, thresholds, and steps get extraheavy wear. They should be painted with a product that is specially formulated to resist abrasion and foot traffic. These paints come in latex and oil-based formulations. They are mixed at the factory in a limited range of colors and gloss levels. These can be combined to create more colors, and small amounts of pigment can even be added, but the range of available colors is limited at best.

Ordinary house paint will not stand up well to being walked on, so use porch and deck paint wherever foot traffic is expected. To improve traction at entrances and on steps, add a small amount of clean sand (available at most paint and hardware stores) to the paint before you apply it.

Porch and deck paint dries much harder than normal paints and primers. For this reason, bare wood that is to be finish coated with porch and deck paint should be primed with porch and deck paint itself rather than with any other material. When used as a primer, porch and deck paint can be thinned slightly to improve its penetrating ability.

Stains

For some wood surfaces you may want to use stain instead of paint. Stains are available in latex and oil-based versions. They are like paint in that they seal the surface and protect it from the weather, but their aesthetic purpose is different. Where paint makes a solid opaque coat on the surface, stains penetrate the surface to reveal the natural color and the physical texture of the wood.

Exterior stains function as a protective coating. They contain the same basic ingredients as house paint (vehicle, pigment, thinning agent, additives) and act in much the same way mechanically. They differ from house paint in their ability to penetrate the surface.

Apply exterior stains in the same way as you apply exterior paints. Take extra care to mix enough stain to do the whole job. Variations in color are more likely with stains than with paints.

The first coat of a transparent or semitransparent stain will show variations in the density of the color in any case. These are caused by variations in the rate of absorption. A second coat can be used to even them out. The sealing action of

Stain Opacity

Clear penetrating sealer on cedar

Semitransparent stain on cedar

Opaque stain on cedar

Same color, different opacity

the first coat makes it easier to control the amount of pigment left on the surface by the second coat.

Stains are ideal for beautifying and protecting woodwork that is too rough textured to prepare for painting. Stains can be applied with very modest surface preparation. There is no need to smooth the surface, to fill nail holes (unless they actually pierce the skin of the building), or to prime. However, stains do not last as long as a properly prepared paint job. This is because they have less build than paints.

Stains weather in the same way as paints. However, when the thin top layer is gone, the wood and the stain that penetrated it begin to weather away together. The solution is simply

to apply another coat of stain. Since this requires no sanding, scraping, filling, or priming, it is relatively painless. Best of all, you will probably need to restain only the most exposed sides of the house. The north side may look good years longer than the west and south sides. Remember to use the same product in the same color when you restain.

Varnishes

Traditional varnishes are resins mixed with a vehicle and dissolved in a solvent. They dry quickly and set clear or slightly amber. The modern equivalents are urethanes, which have a similar composition. Both of these clear coatings have a limited use in exterior house painting. Because they are clear, they offer little or no protection rom ultraviolet light, either to themselves or to the surface under them. Some urethanes have another disadvantage, which is that they dry to an extremely hard, tough finish. As the wood beneath them swells and shrinks in the weather, the urethane will simply delaminate from it. The coating itself may still be intact, but there will be white spots wherever it is no longer attached to the wood.

Spar varnishes were originally intended to protect the wood on ships and boats, so they are a little better suited for exterior use. They are not quite so hard, and they retain some flexibility. Spar varnishes are also destroyed by sunlight and moisture, however. The surface gradually oxidizes, weakens, and flakes off. Use spar varnish on surfaces that are well protected from sun and rain—perhaps a door on a deep porch or gallery.

Varnish is also helpful for keeping new brass and copper bright. If you prefer the patina of weathered copper and brass, varnish the patinated metal. This will keep the oxides in the patina from washing down and staining the wall. Renew the varnish every year.

Penetrating Clear Sealers

Aesthetically, penetrating exterior sealers correspond to transparent interior wood stains. They come in clear or tinted versions. The latter may contain more or less pigment than semitransparent stains. Even the so-called clear versions contain some pigment, though it is not noticeable when the product dries. Penetrating clear sealers are designed for use on new or unfinished wood, or on wood that has been previously treated with the same product. Their pigments will not cover other pigments.

The mechanical function of penetrating clear sealers is to preserve the wood and make it water-repellent. They do this by soaking deep into the wood. The surface film will set dry enough to be dust free in a few hours. Below the surface the sealer takes many months to set. For this reason, sealers are often applied in two coats, wet on wet. This means that the second coat is applied before the first coat has had a chance to set but after it has begun to soak in. This allows the more absorbent areas to soak up as much sealer as they need. Because these products work by curing very slowly, it is important not to apply fresh sealer over sealer that has already set and is no longer absorbent. If you do, the second application will take forever to dry.

Clear and tinted penetrating sealers are oil-based formulations. Techniques and formulations vary from one manufacturer to the next; read the directions on the label carefully. Most sealers can be applied with a brush, a roller, or spray equipment. To prevent buildup, the excess must usually be removed with a dry roller or rags.

Waterproofing Materials

Penetrating clear wood sealers make wood water-repellent for a time, but several other products are designed specifically to waterproof difficult surfaces. Masonry conditioners and sealers are applied in much the same way as wood sealers. They work by soaking into the masonry or concrete, penetrating and filling the cracks that allow moisture to enter.

Elastomeric Sealants

Another broad class of waterproofing materials works differently. Elastomeric sealants are water-based products much like very thick latex paint. When they dry and set, they form a relatively thick coat of very flexible material. The material retains its flexibility for many years and, unlike most latex paints, is impermeable to air and water vapor. Elastomeric sealants are especially useful in treating concrete or stucco walls where the wall itself is fundamentally sound but many small cracks are beginning to appear due to aging. As long as the surface can be made sound, a full coat of elastomeric sealant can stop the water from seeping in without the need to caulk each tiny crack individually. This can be a very great advantage when you must waterproof an entire house.

Elastomeric sealants have a few weaknesses, however. They are even more intolerant of dust, dirt, and chalking surfaces than latex is. If the surface is not perfectly sound, it should be cleaned and primed before the sealant is applied. Because they are impermeable to water vapor, they will also blister badly if water seeps in from behind. They will not crack or peel if they have been properly applied, but the water will cause them to pop off the wall.

Their other drawbacks are more aesthetic than mechanical. Their basic color is usually white or light beige, and because they accept only a small amount of pigment, they come in only a limited range of light tints. Once on they tend to hold dirt more than standard house paints. This can be a problem if they are used as a finish coat on a house near a busy street, for instance. The solution to both of these problems is to use the elastomeric sealant as an intermediate coat between the primer and a latex finish coat. Most of these sealants will make a good foundation for latex, the only danger being that the latex will not be as flexible as the sealant. However, it should be flexible enough for most purposes. In any case, the slight cracking of the finish coat that might be caused by the disparity would be less serious than the alternative, which is water damage.

Because elastomeric sealants are more viscous than latex paints, they cannot be thinned very much. This means that they must be applied with a brush and roller (or with a special spray unit designed for use with mastic). Application and cleanup are the same as for latex with two exceptions. Because the sealant is so thick, use a longer-nap roller cover, and don't expect the sealant to spread as far.

BRUSHING, ROLLING, AND SPRAYING TECHNIQUES

Before applying primer or paint, be sure that the area is properly dropped and masked; that you have all the necessary materials and equipment; that you have prepared the surface properly; and that you have gained safe access.

Getting the Paint on the Wall

The first step is to lay on the paint with the brush or roller. To lay on means simply to get the paint from the bucket onto the house. You can do this any way you like, just so long as the paint gets in the right general location.

Once the paint is on the wall, it must be brushed or rolled out. That is, it must be spread over the area that it is intended to cover. This is often done at right angles to the direction of the brush strokes that will be applied when the area is laid off.

Laying off means making sure that the surface texture of the wet paint looks the way it should. There should be no roller marks; all brush strokes should be even and parallel; and there should be no drips or runs.

Keeping a Wet Edge

Painting must be done in the correct order. This allows the painter to keep a wet edge, which prevents pulling and flashing. Keeping a wet edge means applying wet paint next to wet paint, not next to tacky paint or dry paint.

If a brush or roller is dragged through a section of tacky paint, the paint will pull, and the rough surface will be obvious when it dries. If wet paint is applied next to dry paint, the two applications may dry to a slightly different gloss level. This is known as flashing.

Ideally, paint would be applied to the whole surface at the same instant. Since that is impossible, keeping a wet edge does the next best thing. If you are moving from one side of the object to the other, paint it completely from top to bottom. If you are moving from the top to the bottom, paint it completely from side to side. The limiting factor is the drying time of the paint. The object is to get back to the last starting point (all the way to the top, if you are painting from top to bottom; all the way to the starting side if you are painting from side to side) before the paint gets too tacky to brush out. At any given moment the whole advancing edge of the painted area is wet. As you move along, the paint you applied several passes ago will begin to dry. However, as long as you are keeping a wet edge, the paint will appear to have dried all at once.

Flashing

If you apply fresh paint over dry paint, there will be a line of demarcation between the two applications. Each will seem to have a slightly different sheen, and this will be especially obvious where they meet. This condition is called flashing. If the border between the two applications falls at a natural visual breakpoint, such as at the joint between two pieces of trim, it will be much less noticeable, however.

Flashing is the rule with gloss paints. It can also occur with some low-lustre and dead-flat paints, and—although rarely—with very dark colors.

You may also get flashing if you try to touch up gloss paints or varnishes. The touched-up spot is often invisible from straight ahead, but it has a different sheen when viewed from an angle. This is not so important when you are touching up a window muntin, for example. No one will notice the slight difference in sheen on such a small area. However, don't try to touch up a large, smooth surface, such as a plain door. It is much better to paint the whole door over again.

To avoid flashing, be diligent about keeping a wet edge. This is especially important when you are using gloss paint.

Brushing

It's not hard to use a brush, but it takes a bit of practice. Go slowly at first so you can see what you are doing. Once you get the hang of it, go as fast as you can every now and then. In this way, you will quickly learn what can and can't be done, and you'll have some fun doing it.

Fill a clean, dry 1-gallon or 2-gallon bucket an inch or so deep with paint of the right consistency. It is handy to be able to leave the brush down in the bucket when you need both hands free. If there is too much paint in the bucket, you will drown the brush. If you intend to work from a ladder, make sure you have a good pothook to hang the bucket on. Have a dust brush or a rag with you in case you come across a bit of dust or a spiderweb.

Take a clean, dry brush and dip it into the paint. Under no circumstances should the paint come more than halfway up the bristles. One third of the way up is better. Slap the brush against the inside of the bucket. This removes excess paint and helps to prevent drips. Now you are ready to paint.

To cover a wide, flat area, quickly and crudely lay on the paint, using two quick strokes with the flat of the brush, right side, left side. Don't worry about getting it smooth, or even. Just get it all on the wall in one small area. Now spread the paint out to the right thickness over that area. Don't work yourself or the brush too hard. Apply enough pressure to bend the bristles slightly as you draw the brush along, holding the handle at approximately a 30-degree angle to the surface. Keep the brush strokes even and parallel.

Brushing Technique

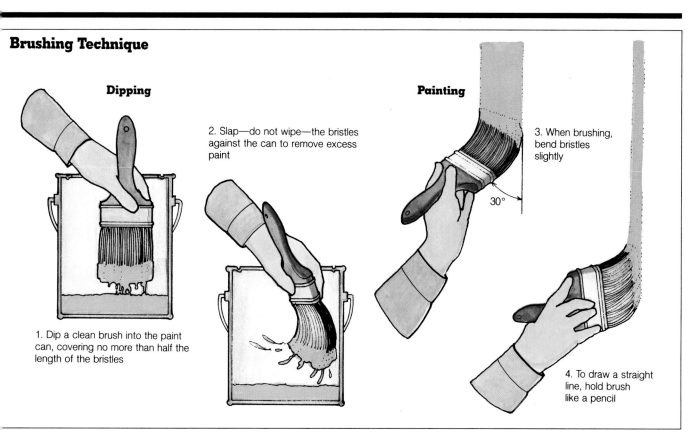

Dipping

2. Slap—do not wipe—the bristles against the can to remove excess paint

1. Dip a clean brush into the paint can, covering no more than half the length of the bristles

Painting

3. When brushing, bend bristles slightly

30°

4. To draw a straight line, hold brush like a pencil

There are correct stroke directions for various construction materials (see page 90) and for doors, windows, and trim (see page 94).

If you are painting a smooth wall, the brush strokes will be most nearly invisible if performed up and down rather than side to side. When you apply flat paint to a textured surface, no one will ever see the brush strokes if the paint is brushed out smoothly in any direction. Don't worry; do what is easiest.

When the first brush full is laid off, dip the brush and begin again. Be sure to lay on the next bit in an unpainted area, not on top of the part that you just brushed out. Brush out the new paint so that it blends smoothly with the bit you just painted.

Brushing a Straight Line

If you are trying to draw, or cut, a straight line, scrape some excess paint off the tips of the bristles on one face of the brush. Do this by gently dragging the brush against the top edge of the bucket. The face of the brush that you clean in this way is the face that will be turned away from the area to be painted.

Place the brush at the top of this area, on the painted side of the imaginary line to be drawn. Apply gentle pressure at first, just allowing the paint to flow from the brush. It will take very little encouragement. All the bristle ends should be just touching the surface. The brush should be aligned so that you can draw it edgewise down

the line, regulating the pressure on the brush to control the flow of paint. Keeping the brush on the to-be-painted side of the line makes it easier to prevent the paint from going over. All you have to do is release the pressure on the bristles. If there is a little too much paint on the brush and it begins to drip, or if the paint threatens to flow over the line, don't panic. Simply move over a bit farther into the to-be-painted zone and quickly draw the brush down parallel to the imaginary line. By now the brush will be much drier. Take it back up to the top of the stroke, pick up any excess paint there, and draw down again, this time closer to or right on the line. There will be enough paint from the first stroke to finish this part of the line.

Slight surface imperfections sometimes make it difficult to get the paint to flow just where you want it to. One solution is to tense the muscles of your hand and arm so that the hand and the brush quiver slightly. This helps the paint to flow off the brush and into the little nooks and crannies. The easiest way to draw a straight line is to drag the brush edgewise. However, this often leaves streaks in the paint. Turn the brush 90 degrees and take out the streaks with the flat of the brush. Because the line is already drawn, this is not very difficult.

Halting Brushing

If you want to stop painting for an hour or so, suspend the brush in the bucket with the bristles in the paint. Don't let it slip down too far. Put the bucket in the shade and cover it to slow evaporation.

If you are quitting for the day but will use the same setup tomorrow, you can wrap the brush in plastic to prevent the paint in it from drying. However, it is better to clean the brush each day, suspend the brush in the cleaning agent, and store it in a cool place.

Rolling

It is faster to apply paint with a roller than with a brush. Rollers have two drawbacks: They leave a distinct texture on the surface, and they are harder to control than brushes. If you paint a flat, smooth surface with a roller, you should brush out the paint immediately to eliminate the roller texture. That said, practically every exterior surface more than 9 inches wide can be painted with a roller.

Rollers throw out paint droplets as they move. This is called roller spray. The faster the roller moves, the longer the nap, and the thinner the material, the more spray. Move the roller more slowly when you are painting at the top of a wall if the eaves above have been completed. Be sure to protect everything below the area where you are rolling.

The basic rolling technique is the same for all materials.

Attach the roller frame to the extension pole, if you are using one. Push the dry roller cover over the frame, making sure that it is well seated. The end of the roller frame should be flush with the end of the roller cover. Fill the tray with enough paint to just begin to cover the lower part of the sloping section. This section serves the same purpose as the screen in a bucket setup. It is used to clean the excess paint off the roller.

Dip the roller in the paint, turning it about to cover it evenly. Roll the roller against the sloping grid of the tray. Continue dipping and rolling until the new roller cover is evenly saturated with paint. Take off the excess paint with a final roll or two. No paint should drip from the roller when you lift it.

Start near, but not at, the top of the wall and lay on this first rollerfull of paint. Roll from the top down. As with brush work, this first laying on just serves to get material onto the wall. You can skip spots, make zigzag patterns, or whatever you want. The important thing is to distribute paint in a more or less balanced way over the area this rollerfull will cover. When you have done this, roll the paint out.

Roll straight up and down over the area where the paint is laid on. The object is to get a smooth, even coat with no holidays, drips, sags, or roller marks.

Roller marks are caused by one of two things. Either you

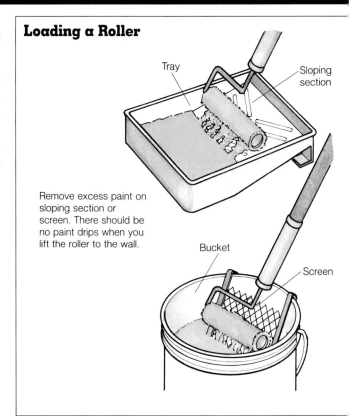

Loading a Roller

Tray

Sloping section

Remove excess paint on sloping section or screen. There should be no paint drips when you lift the roller to the wall.

Bucket

Screen

are pressing down too hard or else there is too much paint built up at the ends of the roller. To clean off the excess, hold the roller at an angle and roll each end in turn against the wall. Then roll out the lines of built-up paint that this creates.

When the roller starts to get too dry to apply an even coat, dip it again and take off the excess as before. Now lay on the paint in the unpainted area adjacent to the one that you just finished. Always roll from the unpainted into the painted. This avoids excess buildup, which causes drips and sags as well as roller marks.

Heavily textured surfaces, especially those which include abrupt changes, such as shingles or a brick wall, promote drips and runs by squeezing excess paint out of the roller. It

is important to get the paint into the recessed areas, but you should go back over your work periodically to pick up the drips and runs with a relatively dry roller and roll them out. Do this before the material becomes tacky.

If you roll into an area that has become tacky, the pull of the paint may not be as noticeable as it would be if you were using a brush. However, the difference in texture will be apparent. Rolling over tacky paint creates what is called orange peel, which is what it resembles. Orange peel is permanent. Depending on the gloss of the finish and the underlying texture of the surface being painted, it may or may not be obvious when the paint dries. If it must be removed,

Roller Technique

1. The roller should be covered with paint but not dripping as you lift it

Extension pole

Roller

Bucket setup

House body

2. Paint, roughly laid-on

3. Paint rolled out in smooth, even coat

you will have to sand it or patch it. Then prepare the surface again and paint it over.

How far will one rollerfull of paint spread? That depends on the nap of the roller, the viscosity and covering ability of the paint, and the texture of the surface to be covered. The longer the nap, the more paint a roller holds. The thinner the paint, and the better it covers, the farther it can be spread. The smoother the surface, the less it takes to coat it. (All the little nooks and crannies in a heavily textured wall represent extra surfaces that must be coated with paint.)

Try to cover an area twice the width of the roller and 4 or 5 feet long with each rollerfull of paint. If this results in too much buildup, spread the paint farther. If you can see the previous coat through the fresh coat, it may be because you are trying to make one rollerful stretch too far. It may also be because the difference in color between old and new paint is too great for one coat to cover, however, so look closely before you decide to put on a thicker coat. The paint must not be applied so thick that it sags, whether it covers or not.

Halting Rolling

When you want to stop for an hour or so, dip the roller to cover it with paint, but don't take off the excess. If you are using a bucket, cover it with a cloth to retard evaporation. Place the bucket setup or the tray in the shade.

If you have finished for today but are sure that you will paint again tomorrow, immerse the roller, frame and all, in paint and cover the bucket or tray with plastic to seal it against evaporation. If you won't paint again for two or three days, remove the roller cover from the handle and immerse it in paint or wrap it in plastic, airtight and clearly labeled. Clean the handle and tray, or the bucket and screen, completely.

Spraying

In using any type of sprayer, assume that anything anywhere near your target will get at least some of the spray. Extensive areas must be protected with drop cloths, and accurate, secure masking is essential. On windy days, especially when you are using slow-drying materials, overspray can drift for a considerable distance, putting plants, cars, and neighboring houses at risk. Use a handheld shield to block overspray when working near the roofline or the corners of the house. This will help to reduce the risk, but you must be very careful to avoid overspraying.

Always wear a canister respirator of a rating approved for the type of material being sprayed. Protect your hair and face from paint by wearing a spray sock. This is a cotton or nylon ski mask. Protect the part of your face not covered by the respirator and the spray sock with a coat of petroleum jelly. This will make cleanup easier, particularly when it comes to your eyelids and eyebrows.

Never point the sprayer at anyone. The jet of paint is under sufficient pressure to inject it under exposed skin. This may not be very painful, but it can cause serious infection. If paint is injected into your skin, seek medical attention immediately.

Spray guns are fitted with a variety of tips. These are graded by the size of the aperture and the width of the fan that the tip is designed to produce. Typical apertures range from .013 inches to .019 inches in diameter. The smaller apertures are used with less viscous materials, such as oil-based enamels. The larger apertures are used with heavier, thicker materials, such as latex house paint. Typical fan widths range from 4 to 18 inches. This is the width of the area that will be painted when the gun is held the correct distance (approximately 12 inches) from the wall. Small fans are used for interior trim work; wide ones for exterior painting. Ask the staff at the place where the equipment was rented to help you choose the best tip for your purpose. If you have bought a handheld pump sprayer and it comes with more than one tip, follow the manufacturer's recommendations for the material and the job at hand.

Airless sprayers are essentially pumps driven by electric motors. They have a feed that sucks up the paint out of the bucket and a pump with adjustable pressure. The paint is pumped through a long hose to a gun. When you pull the trigger, the pressurized paint is forced through the tip at the end of the gun in a fine mist.

To set up the sprayer, start by thinning the material to be sprayed. Follow the manufacturer's instructions. Thin sufficient material to do the entire job or at least one whole section of it. Slight differences in sheen (or very rarely, color) may result from variations in the amount of thinning agent added to the paint. Hold a quart or two of the thinned material in reserve to do touch-ups later.

It is a good idea to strain the paint before using it in a sprayer. Clogged spray tips are a time-consuming nuisance. The only solution is to remove the tip from the gun and clean it in the appropriate thinning agent. Strain the paint and make sure that all in-line filters in the spray equipment are clean if you want to avoid this problem.

Put the strained, thinned material into a 5-gallon bucket. Put the feed of the sprayer into the bucket too.

All pump or airless sprayers must be primed to ready them for spraying. Ask the personnel at the rental agency how to do this, and follow the manufacturer's instructions.

Once the sprayer is primed, adjust the pressure. The pressure, the type of spray tip, and the viscosity of the material determine the pattern of the spray. Use the inside of a cardboard box as the target while you adjust the pressure. Spray the box, holding the gun perpendicular to the surface and about 12 inches away. Observe the pattern made by the spray. Reduce the pressure until fingers appear in the spray pattern. Fingers are extra lines of paint that appear above and below the main pattern when the pressure is too low. Raise the pressure just enough to make the fingers disappear. The pattern should now be one solid band of paint of the width that the tip was designed to deliver. By using the sprayer at the lowest pressure consistent with a good spray pattern, you can reduce overspray to a minimum.

To spray a house correctly, follow four procedures.

• Keep the gun perpendicular to the surface being sprayed. If you hold the gun at an angle, more paint will be delivered to one part of the spray pattern than to another. This will cause drips and runs, and the paint film will be very uneven. If you swing the gun left and right, you will have the same problem. In addition, if the paint is not delivered straight on, any imperfections in the surface will tend to protect whatever is behind them from being painted. This will leave unpainted shadows behind every obstacle.

• Keep the gun the right distance from the surface. If it is held too close, the material will build up too quickly, producing sags, drips, and runs. If it is held too far away, the paint will not form a smooth surface. Instead, you will get a sort of sandy effect as each droplet of paint begins to dry independent of its neighbors.

• Keep the gun moving before, while, and after the trigger is pulled. Sprayers deliver paint at a great rate. If you pull the trigger before the gun is in motion, excess paint will build up at the beginning of the stroke. The same thing will happen at the end of the stroke if you stop moving before you stop spraying.

• Overlap the strokes slightly. A properly adjusted spray pattern is an elongated oval. The sprayer delivers more paint to the center than to the ends of this oval. To get an even film, each pass must slightly overlap the last one.

Use a brush to spread out any drips and runs and to paint areas that are too close to the edge to be painted safely with the sprayer.

When spraying heavily textured surfaces, use a roller to work in the paint immediately after you apply it with the sprayer. Where the shape of a surface obliges you to spray it from different angles (as with board siding or split shingles, for example), it is best to spray two light mists by moving the gun faster and slightly farther away from the surface than usual. This prevents excess buildup. Examine the surface carefully; there should be enough paint to make a solid film but not so much that drips and runs appear.

Halting Spraying

If you want to stop spraying for an hour or two, set the sprayer and the gun in the shade. Cover the paint and the gun with a cloth to slow evaporation. To stop overnight, if you are sure that you will work with the same material the next day, simply immerse the tip end of the gun in the appropriate thinning agent and cover the paint. If you are using a handheld pump sprayer, it is best to clean it out each night.

Cleaning Sprayers

To clean a handheld pump sprayer, follow the manufacturer's instructions.

To clean a piston or diaphragm pump airless sprayer, take the feed out of the paint and put it into a 5-gallon bucket containing at least 2 gallons of the appropriate thinning agent. Reprime the machine if necessary. Remove the tip from the gun and drop it into a clean bucket filled with the appropriate thinning agent. Pump the paint that is in the machine and in the line into the bucket containing the paint that you were using. Be careful not to splash the paint; the pressure will be very high when the trigger is first pulled. When the paint becomes noticeably thinner, stop spraying into the bucket. This means that the thinning agent is starting to come through the line. Pump the thinning agent back into the bucket that is supplying the pump. Replace the dirty thinning agent with clean and run this through the machine. Do this two or three times until the material coming through the gun looks reasonably clean. Clean the tip by sloshing it around in the appropriate thinning agent; use a toothbrush, if necessary, to remove any paint residue. Replace the tip. Turn the machine off and relieve the pressure on it, then close the valve that you opened to relieve the pressure. When you take the sprayer back to the rental agency, tell them whether there is water or paint thinner in it and let them take it from there.

Do not overlook the small details when painting. The front fence of this house, also pictured on page 76, was planned to complement the paint design, as was the arbor in the side yard.

The walls, or house body, are usually painted before you paint the windows, doors, and trim. The basic techniques are the same whether you are applying primers or paints. However, different construction materials require slightly different approaches.

Plan of Attack

Primers and finish coats are applied in the same manner. However, primers can be applied on an as-needed basis. There are a few general rules in applying the finish coat.

• Work from the top down and the inside out. This way, you are less likely to mess up completed work by dripping paint on it.

• Apply flat paints before gloss paints. If there are any drips of paint in the wrong place, it is easier to touch up the flat than to touch up the gloss. Leave areas to be stained to be finished last. It is easier to sand out paint drips before staining.

• Reach a visual breakpoint before you stop. This is particularly important with gloss finishes, so plan the workday accordingly.

• Keep drying times in mind when you plan your work. Paint doors and first-floor windows early in the day so that you can close them and replace the locks before dark.

• If you are using more than one color in the same day, consider how long it will take the first color to dry. It must be dry before you can paint a second color next to it.

• In summer plan the job so that you will not be working in the sun. You may enjoy working in direct sunlight, but fresh paint and the noonday summer sun make a bad combination.

• Pace yourself. Overexertion on Saturday and painful recovery on Sunday will not get the project finished. Find the level of effort that is right for you. Break the job into small segments and do them one at a time. Enjoyment and a sense of progress are the rewards of good planning.

• Wear a long-sleeved shirt, a hat, and eye protection to minimize personal cleanup. Paint can be difficult to remove from skin and hair. Use sunscreen to protect yourself from hours of UV exposure.

Horizontal Boards and Smooth Siding

Horizontal boards, often called clapboards, and other smooth sidings are common in residential construction. Use a 7-inch roller to lay the paint on quickly. Be careful not to lay on more than you can brush out before it begins to pull.

Painting Horizontal Board Siding

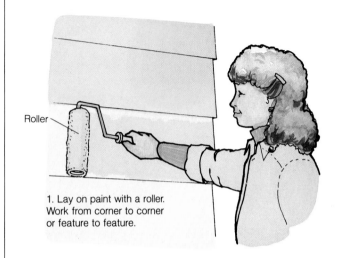
Roller

1. Lay on paint with a roller. Work from corner to corner or feature to feature.

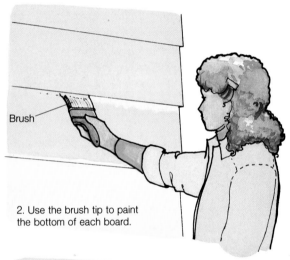
Brush

2. Use the brush tip to paint the bottom of each board.

3. Using horizontal strokes, brush out the paint.

Repeat steps for each section

Once the paint is laid on, use a brush to paint the bottom edge of a clapboard or piece of smooth siding first, then paint its face. Work from the top down, painting a group of as many clapboards as you can conveniently reach and still keep a wet edge. Paint each group of clapboards from corner to corner, or from one corner to some other stopping place, such as a window or door. Stroke horizontally. Look over the work from time to time and brush out any runs or drips. It is common for the bottom edge of siding to pick up extra paint.

Brick and Stucco

Rollers are generally preferred for painting masonry surfaces. They are faster than brushes, and the texture they impart is not noticeable in the heavy texture of the masonry. However, masonry can be painted with a rough-surface painter.

Even with a very long-nap roller, some areas will probably have to be touched up with a brush if the surface is very heavily textured. Check the work periodically for drips; the heavy texture can retain excess

Carefully mask prefinished surfaces, such as the gutters and rails of this International house, before painting. All horizontal boards are painted using the same methods, whether they are clapboards, which overlap, or are set tight, as here.

paint. Go over the drips while they are still wet using a relatively dry brush or roller.

Shakes and Shingles

Paint, stain, and clear sealers can be applied with a brush, a brush and roller, a sprayer, a rough-surface painter, or a shingle brush. If you use a roller, expect a lot of drips. Have a brush handy to remove them and to paint the spots the roller cannot reach. The surface of the shingles is too rough to justify brushing out the roller texture. The texture of split shingles, with their many parallel grooves, is particularly difficult when they are new. A rough-surface painter is the ideal tool here.

Vertical Board and Batten

Board-and-batten siding consists of flat, smooth boards running vertically with the joints between them covered by narrow strips of wood (battens).

Board and batten is painted in the same way as clapboard except that the brush strokes should be vertical rather than horizontal.

Texture 1-11 and Patterned Siding

Many modern houses are covered with exterior plywood that has grooves cut in it to simulate individual boards. The best known of these products is called Texture 1-11 siding. It

usually has a rough, rustic surface, which calls for a roller. Use a roller cover with a ¾-inch nap and work the paint into the surface a little to make sure that it covers completely. Use a brush only to cut in and to finish the grooves, which may fill up with excess paint. The brush will pick it up and spread it out.

Composition Siding and Shingles

Siding and shingles made of composed materials—including asbestos—were long popular for covering wood-frame houses. The thin, stiff plates have a slightly rough texture. They are very brittle, so take care when replacing or resetting loose nails.

Use a roller with a ½-inch nap to apply paint to composition siding or shingles. There is no need to brush out the roller texture. Use a brush to cut in and to make sure that areas of overlap are covered. As with any shingles or siding, excess paint can build up in these areas. Brush out any drips or runs.

Note: Composition siding is perfectly safe when it is firmly attached to the side of a house. However, asbestos fibers are very dangerous if they are inhaled. Do not sand or do anything to asbestos siding that will abrade it and create asbestos dust. Badly deteriorated siding should be removed by a professional contractor specializing in asbestos removal.

Painting Shingle Siding

1. Hold rough-surface painter with gap towards bottom. Apply paint with vertical strokes.

2. Use the small set of bristles to paint bottom of shingles.

3. An extension pole can be attached to most shingle brushes.

Different surfaces require different painting equipment and techniques. This Victorian has a combination of sidings. Use a roller and a flat wall brush for the first-story stucco, a special shingle brush for the intricate shingles, and an angled sash brush for the trim.

Painting features—windows, doors, and trim—is usually the last, most challenging, and most rewarding part of painting a house. The techniques for each feature differ slightly with the design. The most common designs are described here.

Face Off Versus Wrap

The first thing to do in painting a window, a door, or any other piece of trim is to decide how much of it will be painted in the body color and how much in the trim color. It is slightly more common to carry up the body color to cover the outside edge of the feature. The trim color is applied to the face and the inside edges only. This is called facing off the feature.

The other alternative is to paint not only the face of the piece but also the edge that is next to the body with the trim color. This is called wrapping the color on the feature. In many cases, it is very difficult to do this and still create a smooth, straight line of demarcation between the body color and the trim color.

In either case, start by painting the outside edge of the feature. It is difficult to do this without getting some paint on

the face. Be ready to wipe this paint away, unless you are going to lay on and brush out the face immediately.

Painting Windows

Windows are made in three basic styles: sash, or guillotine models; casement models, which open like doors; and fixed models, which do not open at all. Sash windows are the commonest and the most complicated to paint. The techniques for painting other windows are variations on the basic sash techniques.

Sash Windows

To paint a sash window, unlock it and open it slightly from the inside. Slide the upper half down and the lower half up

past the upper half to expose the upper part of the lower half of the window, which will be painted first.

Paint in this order: the upper rail, the upper parts of the side stiles, and the upper parts of any muntins or crossbars on this lower half. Slide the parts of the window back toward their normal positions, but do not close the window. You want to expose the wet edge of the painting you just did, so that you can finish the lower window. Finish painting the lower window: muntins, lower rail, and side stiles. You may need to paint a little more of the side stiles partway through this process to keep the edges wet (see page 84). Now paint the very bottom of the bottom rail of the top window. Be careful not to

Painting Order for Windows

Open the window from the inside by sliding the upper half down and the lower half up

Without closing, slide the window back toward normal position, exposing the just-painted edge

put more paint on the side stiles of the bottom window as you do this. They will be quite close together. Paint the rest of the top window: muntins, top and bottom rails, and side stiles.

If the window frame and sill are to be painted the same color as the sashes, do this next. Start with the top of the frame. Paint the inside (closest to the sash) first; then the face. Do the same for the sides of the frame—insides first, then the faces. Be careful not to hit the sashes, which may be tacky by now. Don't build up paint between the frame and the sash; it will interfere with opening and closing the window. Paint the sill, remembering that the bottom is visible from below.

If the window frame and sill are to be painted in more than one color, wait until the first color dries before you apply the next. The painting order remains the same.

Casement Windows

Paint casements in this order: exposed edge, muntins, top of sash, bottom of sash, sides of sash, and frame. Casement windows, like doors, have edges that show when they are open. The general rule is that these edges should be painted in the color of the area from which they will be visible. Paint these edges first; then proceed in the same order as for sash windows. When painting edges, have a rag handy to wipe off any stray paint that may get on the inside surface of the window.

It is very popular to paint windows and doors with more than one color, as exemplified by the blue and red trim paint on this shingle house. Always allow the first color to dry completely before applying the second color. The painting order remains the same no matter how many different colors are used.

Painting a Flush Door

1. Open door. Paint hinge edge. Wipe the face clean.

2. Roughly lay on paint to the top left third of the door face.

3. Without putting on more paint, brush out the same section horizontally.

4. Lay off paint to same section using parallel vertical strokes.

5. Paint the rest of the door using the same methods.

Fixed Windows

The order in which to paint a fixed window is muntins, top of sash, bottom of sash, sides of sash, and frame. Otherwise painting a fixed window is identical to painting a casement window that doesn't open.

Painting Doors

Doors have edges that are visible only when the door is open. Paint these edges in the color appropriate to the area from which they will be seen. A similar logic applies to painting the frame. Stand on the side of the door that has the stop, pull the door toward you, and close it. The part of the stop that is visible when the door is closed should be painted the same color as the rest of the frame that is visible from that side. The part of the stop that is hidden when the door is closed should be painted the same color as the other side of the doorframe.

If the door has simple hardware, cover it with masking tape, especially if you intend to lay on the paint with a roller. If the hardware is complex and difficult to paint around, remove it temporarily.

Flat or Flush Doors

First, paint the edge that is visible when the door is open. Wipe off any paint that rolls over onto the other side. Start in the upper left-hand corner of the door and lay on the paint with a few quick strokes.

Spread the paint over this section with the flat of the brush, moving from side to side. Be careful not to scrape the bristles over the top or the side edge of the door, creating a puddle of paint there. Lay on and spread out a bit more paint in the same way on the upper right-hand part of the door, so that the whole top quarter of the door is covered with an even coat of paint. Now take a nearly dry brush and, starting in the unpainted area just below the painted area, drag the flat of the brush straight up through the paint to leave an even series of smooth, parallel brush strokes running straight up and down. Do this all the way along. Paint each quarter of the door in the same manner.

Cut in around the door handle before you lay off. To lay off, place the nearly dry tips of the bristles right next to the hardware and stroke either up or down, but not side to side. When you get to the bottom, be careful not to scrape paint off the brush onto the bottom edge of the door.

You have to be quick when painting a door. Keep a wet edge, or the paint will start to pull. If obvious imperfections occur, either scrape off the paint before it sets and try again (a very messy proposition at best) or wait until the paint dries, sand out the imperfections, and start over.

Paneled Doors

Paint the appropriate edge, then the molding around the first panel, then the first panel itself, then the molding around the second panel, then the second panel itself, and so forth until all the moldings and panels have been painted. Next, paint any vertical areas between the panels, the horizontal areas between the panels, the top rail, the bottom rail, the hanging stile on the hinge side, and the closing stile on the latch side.

Be careful not to let paint pool in the corners of the moldings. If this happens put the tip of a fairly dry brush into the corner and pull out the excess paint. Brush strokes should be even and parallel. There should be no obvious stops and starts in the middle of a piece.

To lay off recessed panels, put the tips of the bristles at one end of the panel and pull out from the molding, dragging the brush about two thirds of the way along the panel. Then go to the opposite end of the panel, put the tips of the bristles against the molding, and pull back the other way. Gradually lift the brush from the surface as this second stroke comes down over the first one.

Brush strokes should follow the grain of the wood. Stroke up and down on the stiles, side to side on the rails, up and down on the panels if they are divided vertically and side to side if they run the width of the door. Make straight, crisp divisions between areas of horizontal brush strokes and areas of vertical brush strokes in the same plane. The stiles extend the whole length of the door

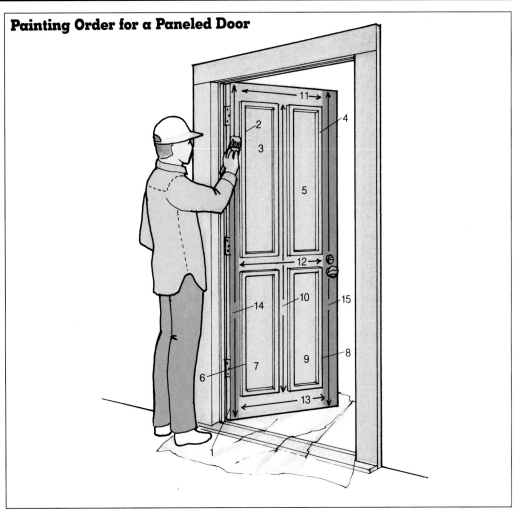

Painting Order for a Paneled Door

and cut off the rails. In divisions between the panels, horizontals cut off verticals.

Roll-Up Garage Doors

Garage doors that roll up are painted like other panel doors with one exception. Each section of the door has an edge that becomes visible for a moment as the door opens or closes. Unless the door is disassembled, these edges cannot be painted all at once. They must be painted in batches.

Paint the first section. Then open the door enough to expose the first edge to be painted. (You might need to disconnect the door closer from the track, usually a simple matter of pulling a small lever. To reconnect it, push the lever back.) Paint the exposed edges, then the next panel. Open the door a little farther and repeat the process. Do this until you see that your next move is going to push together two freshly painted edges. At this point quit. Go do something else until the first application of paint has had a chance to

dry. Then continue. When you stop, stop at an edge, not a panel. Otherwise excess paint will build up in the narrow gap between the panels when the door is closed.

Painting Louvers

Louvers designed for ventilation are built with the weather side out. That is, the lower edge of each louver is closer to the outside of the house.

To paint both the weather side and the inside of louvers, open the louvers, paint the inside, quickly close the louvers, and brush out the drips that

Painting Order for Louvers

Paint shutters, such as these umber ones, after the house body. Use the techniques that are used to paint ventilation louvers. Spread a drop cloth to protect surrounding surfaces and watch out for drips and slips.

will certainly have appeared on the weather side. Then paint the weather side.

To minimize these drips dip an angle sash brush about an inch into the paint. Gently slap the side of the brush against the inside of the bucket to remove some of the excess. Starting at the top right, dab some of the paint into the corner where the louver goes into the frame. Distribute this first brush full of paint between the right-hand ends of the first two to four louvers (depending on their size). Dip the brush again and do the same for the left side of this first set of louvers. Try to paint the inside edge of the frame up between the louvers without scraping paint off the brush on the inside edge of the louvers. Dip the brush deeper this time, picking up a little more paint. Crudely lay it on the first louver or two; then brush it out, side to side. When the paint is well spread out, lay off as follows. Put the tip of the fairly dry brush into the corner at one extreme end of the top louver, laying the flat of the brush on its surface. Pull the brush out of the corner, bringing any excess paint with it. Do the same thing at the opposite end of the same louver. Now move down to the next louver and repeat.

Paint the inside of the frame between the louvers first. Then paint the main length of the louvers, one or two at a time, finishing each louver by pulling the excess paint out of the corners. Most of the drips and runs in painting louvers occur at the point where they meet the frame. You paint this part first so that any drips will show up while you can still deal with

them conveniently. Finish by painting the frame. Follow the techniques used for window frames. Remember to check for additional drips as the paint dries. If you have used oil-based paint, they may not appear for hours.

Painting Railings

It's hard to keep a wet edge when you paint railings. It is best if two people can work together, painting both sides of the railing at the same time. If you must do the job alone, do the far side first, then the side closer to you, and then the top of the handrail.

Start at one end of the railing and paint the balusters, on all sides if possible. Don't forget the undersides of curlicues and details. Don't scrape the paint off the brush on the railing; this causes drips and runs. Clean excess paint out of corners and details by placing the tip of the nearly dry brush in the corner and pulling out. When you paint the second side, remember that any excess paint that rolls over onto the first side may flash. If the first side is still tacky when you paint the second side, drips and runs may be impossible to brush out.

Picking Out Details

Emphasize interesting trim details by painting them in a contrasting color or even in several colors. All other things being equal, save the color that covers best for last.

Painting Railings

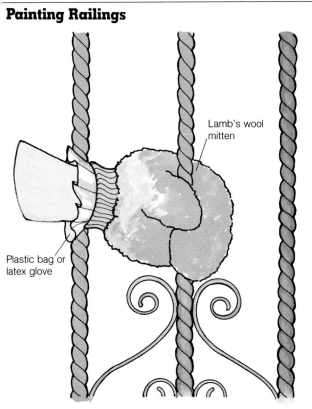

Lamb's wool mitten

Plastic bag or latex glove

Dip mitten in paint until soaked but not dripping. Wipe against rails using smooth motion. Clean mitten after use following directions for a roller cover (see page 104). Liner prevents paint from getting on painter's hand.

The general rule is to paint from the inside out. This rule is reversed in doing certain kinds of detailing. If there is a decorative V groove in a fascia, it is easier to paint the whole fascia first and then go back and paint the groove in a contrasting color. However, if the groove is square in cross-section, it is probably easier to paint the groove first.

To paint a complex raised carving, such as a garland, in a contrasting color, paint the garland first and then cut back with the color of the flat background. It is easier to control the brush on a flat surface than on a curved one.

Often, however, the general rule still applies. If you have a repetitive pattern or a relatively shallow carving or relief, paint the whole piece with the background color. When this is dry, dip the brush in the contrasting color and scrape most of the paint from the brush. Drag the tip of this nearly dry brush over the face of the carving, just hitting the tops of the details very lightly. It's a bit like making a rubbing of a carved stone. When you pick out the details this way, be very careful not to have too much paint on the brush. Drips and runs will spoil the effect completely. When the details are thoroughly defined, go back carefully over any areas where the contrasting color is thin or streaky.

Painting Trim

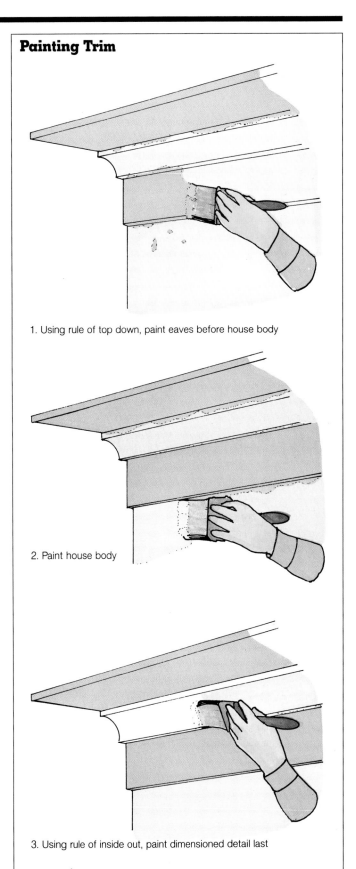

1. Using rule of top down, paint eaves before house body

2. Paint house body

3. Using rule of inside out, paint dimensioned detail last

USING MATERIALS OTHER THAN PAINT

Stains, waterproofing materials, clear sealers, varnishes, and urethanes are all used in exterior house painting. Most are applied with the same tools and techniques as are used for paint. However, there are a few differences.

Stains

Exterior stains are applied in exactly the same way as exterior paints of the same vehicle. Semitransparent stains may need two applications over new wood or previously unfinished wood to achieve a perfectly even color.

Waterproofing Materials

Heavy-bodied elastomeric sealants are applied like other latex paint. However, because they are heavier and more viscous than paint, they require a roller with at least a ¾-inch nap, and they will not spread nearly as far as paint. Set up the roller in a 5-gallon bucket with a screen. These materials are too thick to use conveniently from a tray.

Clear Sealers

Clear penetrating sealers come in oil-based and oil-modified emulsion formulations. Each proprietary product is applied a little differently, so follow the manufacturer's instructions. Generally, these products can be applied with a brush or with a roller. If they are sprayed on, they must usually be rolled into the surface. Often, two coats are applied wet on wet to increase the amount of the material and improve the evenness of the absorption. All of these products are relatively slow drying

below the surface, so don't apply a fresh coat over a cured coat. This can create puddles of unset material.

Varnishes and Urethanes

There are many different solvent-based urethanes and varnishes. Generally, these products dry much faster than paint. They dry so quickly, in fact, that rapid, accurate, and accomplished brushwork is required to apply a smooth, even coat to an area as large as a flush door. Objects with more natural visual breakpoints require slightly less speed, but greater accuracy and planning, for satisfactory results with a brush. Many varnishes can dry to the point where they begin to pull in a few minutes.

Do not use solvent-based varnishes and urethanes with rollers or with handheld, airless, or diaphragm pump sprayers. Follow the manufacturer's recommendations for thinning and cleanup.

Varnishing Flush Doors

When you varnish a flush door, begin with the edge as for painting (see page 96), but make sure that the material does not roll over onto either face of the door. Next, varnish the face, beginning at the extreme upper left side, but instead of working across, work straight down from top to bottom in an area one brush width wide or a little more. Do not cross-brush the material. Lay

Cape Cod houses like this are traditionally stained gray to achieve the weathered-by-the-sea look of the Massachusetts coast, where the architectural style was first popularized.

Top: The simple lines of a saltbox house lend themselves to a simple two-toned paint design. You can use the same equipment to apply stain—like the beige stain on this house body—and trim paint, but be sure to clean the brushes thoroughly between products.
Bottom: Varnish is a good choice for a door made from high-quality wood because it allows the grain to show through. However, varnish does not protect as well as paint. It should be used only on doors like this one that are not exposed to the elements.

on, brush out, and lay off the varnish with up-and-down strokes in this one narrowly defined area. Lay off the last work at the bottom and get back to the top before the first bit becomes tacky. Varnish the next strip in the same way, blending it in with the edge of the previous strip. Be careful not to build up excess material. Keep the coat as thin as you can and still cover without leaving holidays. Continue working across the door in thin strips. Cut in around any hardware as for painting, but keep in mind that varnish is drippier than paint. Be careful not to build up excess material around hardware and knobs or along edges.

If you need to apply a second coat, follow the manufacturer's instructions with respect to drying times. If there are any drips, runs, or sags in the first coat, sand them out

when you rough up the surface. A well-applied second coat should make them disappear. With some formulations varnish applied over varnish becomes tacky faster than varnish applied over bare wood.

Varnishing Paneled Doors

To varnish a paneled door, follow the same order as for painting (see page 97), but with the following exceptions. Do not cross-brush varnish; there is no time and no need. When you varnish one section or one piece, cover it completely, laying off any excess material cleanly. Define each piece sharply; don't let any material spill over onto areas that will be varnished later. This prevents pulling and excess buildup.

PAINTING SPECIAL EFFECTS

House painting need not be limited to plain, solid colors. You can imitate natural materials or create interesting patterns as well. Mastery of the more complex techniques is reserved for the skilled artisan, but mastery of the basic elements allows anyone to create strikingly beautiful effects on any house.

Marbleizing

Artist's brush to draw veins

Rounded sponge to remove excess paint

Dry brush to feather veins

Sponging

A sponged, or mottled, finish is most typically applied over stucco, using earth tones to simulate natural stone. The sponging process will soften the colors so that much darker shades can be used without looking heavy or oppressive. Use latex paints for sponged effects.

Choose a dark base color and a lighter second color. Use a roller to apply the base color to as much of the surface as can be conveniently sponged in half an hour. Before the base coat dries, use a large rounded sponge to apply the second color. The irregular shapes of organic sponges work best for this. Dip the sponge in the paint. Then, using a tapping motion, set it directly onto the painted surface. Do not drag it. Partially blend the second color into the base coat, forming random patterns of irregular shapes and sizes. Be sure to rinse out the sponge between paint dips, because it will pick up much of the base color. When the area is finished, step back to check out the overall pattern. Keep it simple, especially if you plan to cover a large area. Sponged techniques are most effective if the whole area is finished in the same general pattern.

Marbleizing

If you want to use paint to imitate natural marble, you will need a sample of marble from which to work. You will also need appropriate amounts of oil-based paint for each of the colors in the sample. The surface to be marbleized should be very smooth. Apply a base coat of light-value oil-based paint, being careful not to leave any brush marks. Let it dry thoroughly.

Mix up a thin glaze coat of 2 parts oil-based paint to 1 part thinner to match the color of one of the darker values of the sample. Brush the glaze over an area. Then gently use a dry rounded sponge to break up the surface.

With an artist's brush, put in the larger veining strokes across the wet glazed surface. Study the sample for the look of natural veins. Veining lines should be irregular, meandering diagonally and breaking off to the left and to the right. As in real marble, each painted vein should have an end and a beginning. Lines should not suddenly appear and then fade out again.

Using a dry sponge, carefully touch up veins to remove excess paint. With a clean, dry brush, feather out the veins

by working lightly along in one direction and then the other, softening and blurring the edges of veining into the surrounding glaze color. Now, using a darker color, paint in the small veins that link the large ones together. Sponge lightly again and soften with a clean, dry brush. Add some lighter veins to bring out more depth.

When the entire surface is thoroughly dry, apply a coat of low-sheen polyurethane or spar varnish for protection. As a finishing touch, buffing with superfine 400-grit sandpaper will help to give the surface of the dry varnish the look of real marble.

Wood Graining

This section describes the basic technique for using paint to imitate natural wood. Commercial

graining tools and kits are also available. These come with complete instructions.

Wood graining requires certain special tools. These can be improvised, or they can be had at reasonable prices from some paint stores and many art supply houses. The most common tool is called a graining comb. This device looks something like a metal hair comb that has been run over by a steamroller, the teeth are wide and flat and there are substantial gaps, sometimes of varying size, between them. The ends of the teeth are cut square and perfectly even. Graining combs can be improvised from relatively tough, slightly flexible plastic (such as a heavy plastic bottle) cut into shape with a matte knife.

Stenciling

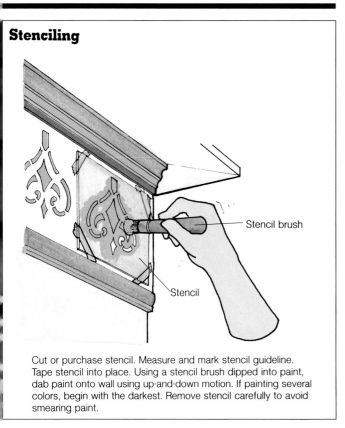

Cut or purchase stencil. Measure and mark stencil guideline. Tape stencil into place. Using a stencil brush dipped into paint, dab paint onto wall using up-and-down motion. If painting several colors, begin with the darkest. Remove stencil carefully to avoid smearing paint.

Stencil brush

Stencil

Just how many windows decorate the side of this yellow stucco house? Three and a figment of a housepainter's imagination. Special effects can take many forms. Only your imagination limits the choice.

To wood grain a flat door-frame, you will need a drop cloth, buckets, a 2-inch or 3-inch brush for applying the paint, an artist's pencil or a small round brush for drawing in the grain, a soft brush for mottling the edges (an old brush will do), and one or more graining tools.

Use oil-based paints and choose good brushes. Have a supply of clean rags and paint thinner on hand.

Start by finding a good example of the wood to be imitated. Observe the pattern of the grain. Notice the different colors in the wood, how they vary from light to dark in a sinuous but somehow regular pattern.

Choose the predominant light color as the base. The piece to be grained must be as smooth as possible before you apply the base coat. Give it a complete, even coat of the base color and let the paint dry thoroughly.

Mix up a small amount of the predominant dark color. If the sample contains highlights of a lighter color than the base, make up a small amount of this color as well.

Mix 2 parts of the dark paint with 1 part of thinner to make a glaze. Apply this glaze in a thin, streaky coat over one entire piece to be grained. Put the teeth of the graining comb at one end of the piece and drag it along, raking away the freshly applied glaze to reveal the base coat underneath. Move the comb this way and that, changing the angle to change the width of the streaks you are creating. Wiggle the comb a little to imitate the pattern of the grain. Use a finer comb to get the finer grain patterns at the edge of an area. Leave room for features that are easier to draw in with the artist's pencil, such as knots. Clean the glaze from these areas with a rag wrapped around your finger, if necessary. If you don't like the effect, wipe it off with thinner and a rag. Wait a bit and start over. It's difficult to get it perfect the first time. Just be patient and keep experimenting.

When you achieve the grain pattern you want, let the glaze set up for just a few minutes. Then take a soft, dry brush and drag it in one direction only along the grain pattern to imitate the way the darker color trails off into the lighter one.

The object is to pick up a tiny bit of the glaze and spread it out to one side of the individual streaks. Draw in any knots or other details and soften any edges with the dry brush as needed. Any lighter areas can be added now. However, if they must also be softened and spread out with a dry brush, don't add them until the darker glaze has set.

Remember to follow the structure of a real piece of wood. Remember too that you must clearly mark the boundaries between one piece of imitation wood and the next.

Half an hour spent cleaning up equipment—and yourself—tonight will save you that much more time tomorrow. When the project is completed, cleaning the site properly will give the house a truly finished look. Don't forget to store and dispose of leftover materials in an environmentally sound way.

Cleaning the Equipment

Keep your equipment in good working order if you want to paint easily and well. This means keeping brushes, rollers, buckets, roller trays, and screens scrupulously clean. A wire brush is nearly essential for cleaning brushes and a brush comb is very useful too. A curved tool for cleaning rollers comes in handy if you plan to use the same roller cover for more than one type of material.

Different products require different cleaning agents. In the case of latex paints, this is water. In the case of oil-based paints, it is paint thinner. In the case of alkyd-modified latex paints, the cleanup is done with water followed by a final rinse in thinner. Some solvent-based products can be cleaned with paint thinner even though they cannot be thinned with it. A very few products must be cleaned with alcohol. Always follow the instructions on the product label.

The basic procedures described next apply to every kind of product. Procedures specific to oil-based, latex, and solvent-based products begin on page 106.

Canning the Paint

Pour the paint from the buckets and the roller tray back into the appropriate storage containers. If you have a brush that was in the same material that you are pouring, use it to scrape out the tray or bucket. A brush covered in different material will contaminate the paint. If you plan to reuse the roller sleeve, stand it on end in the roller tray or braced against the top of the screen in the bucket and scrape down the excess paint. Put this last bit of paint into the storage container.

Note: When you scrape the paint from a roller cover, a bit of nap may come with it. If the paint is glossy, either discard it or strain before reuse.

Cleaning the Roller Cover

Put the roller in a 5-gallon bucket and force the cleaning agent down into the cover nap. Remove the dissolved paint by scraping along the side of the roller cover with a curved tool or by using your hands with a slight wringing action. Pour a

Cleaning Latex from Roller Covers

1. Milk excess paint from cover into paint tray

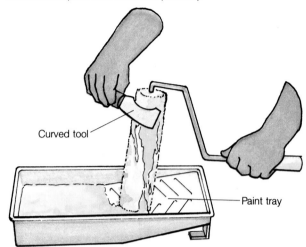

Curved tool

Paint tray

2. Working under running water, wring until clean

3. Spin dry

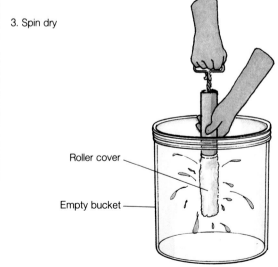

Roller cover

Empty bucket

Cleaning Brushes

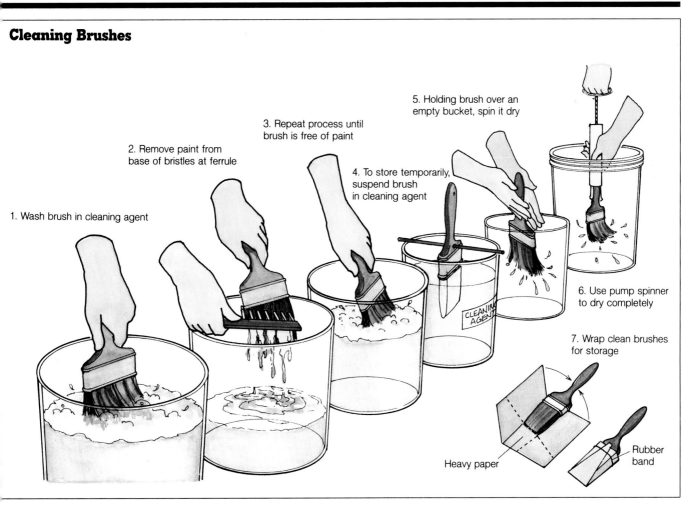

1. Wash brush in cleaning agent

2. Remove paint from base of bristles at ferrule

3. Repeat process until brush is free of paint

4. To store temporarily, suspend brush in cleaning agent

5. Holding brush over an empty bucket, spin it dry

6. Use pump spinner to dry completely

7. Wrap clean brushes for storage

CLEANING AGENT

Heavy paper

Rubber band

thin stream of agent onto the roller cover periodically as you work the dirty agent out. Continue until the cleaning agent runs almost clear. Then spin out the excess as follows. Put the cover partway over the roller frame. Spin the cage with your hand, holding the assembly in such a way that the cover is suspended vertically in the air in the middle of the 5-gallon bucket. Leave the roller cover partially on the roller frame and set this assembly aside to dry, propping the handle so that the roller cover is straight up-and-down, not leaning against or touching

anything. If any part of it does touch something, that part will collect the last bits of material in the roller and will dry hard.

Cleaning the Brushes

Hold the flat of the brush against the edge of the paint collection bucket and use a wire brush to clean out the paint in the heel (the point where the bristles disappear into the ferrule). Paint buildup here can ruin the responsiveness of a brush. Hold the brush in your left hand, steadying it on the edge of the bucket but providing all the support yourself. With the wire brush in

your right hand, push from the ferrule toward the ends of the bristles. Turn the paintbrush over and repeat.

Pour a few inches of cleaning agent into a container. Place the brush in the cleaning agent and work it back and forth to force the agent through the bristles. Don't force the bristles down. Keep them parallel as they would be when painting. Bend them more than you would when painting, but make sure that they all bend the same way at the same time.

Put an inch or two of cleaning agent in another container and repeat the process. Repeat with fresh cleaning agent until no more pigment comes from the bristles.

To remove the excess cleaning agent from the clean brush, hold the handle between your palms and, with the brush hanging in midair, spin it by rubbing your palms back and forth a few times. If you are using paint thinner as a cleaning agent, spin the brush in the middle of a clean 5-gallon bucket to avoid splashing thinner on yourself or the house.

After each brush is spun, make sure that your hands are

clean and gently reshape the bristles. If the bristles are not perfectly parallel, comb them out with a brush comb or brush them out with a clean wire brush before shaping.

Put each brush back in its keeper or wrap it in newspaper. This keeps the bristles from splaying out as they dry. Do not crimp the brush or bend the bristles when you put it away. If you do, the bend will be permanent.

Cleaning Oil-Based Materials

All oil-based materials must be cleaned with paint thinner. Follow the basic procedures outlined above.

To clean the buckets, roller tray, and roller handle, start with used paint thinner, if you have any. Pour several inches of it into one of the larger buckets. Use one of the brushes to clean the sides of the bucket. Scrape the bottom as well. Set this brush aside. Put the next brush in the bucket and gently work it around, pushing the bristles over first to one side and then to the other. Pour off the thinner into the next bucket and repeat the process.

Pour some thinner from this second bucket into the roller tray. Use a little less than you would if the thinner were paint. Using one of the brushes, apply thinner to the roller handle to dissolve any paint. Wipe the handle clean with a rag and set it aside to dry. Working gently, dissolve the paint in the tray as you did for the buckets. By now the

thinner will be full of paint, so you may not be able to get the tray very clean. Pour the thinners from the tray and the second bucket into the 5-gallon bucket. Pour a few inches of clean or nearly clean thinner into the first bucket. Take the first brush and clean the bucket again. Pour the thinner into the second bucket, wipe out the first bucket with a rag, and set it aside to dry. Pour thinner from the second bucket into the roller tray as before and clean the tray completely. Finish by pouring the excess thinner into the 5-gallon bucket and wiping out the tray with a rag.

Cleaning Latex Materials

Use water to clean up latex or other water-based materials. Follow the basic procedure for cleaning brushes and roller covers. Wash buckets, screens, and handles in a utility sink. Use warm or cold water; hot water tends to set the paint. Use the brushes to clean the buckets and tray.

Cleaning Alkyd-Modified Latex Materials

Start by cleaning the equipment thoroughly with water. When it is as clean as you can get it, there will still be a sticky residue. Spin the water out of the brushes and the roller cover and wipe the buckets dry. Pour a few inches of clean paint thinner into one of the buckets and wash all brushes and roller covers in this. Replace the dirty thinner with an inch or so of clean thinner and rinse everything again, brushes first.

This time the thinner should be relatively clean. Dip the corner of a clean rag into it and wipe out the other buckets and the roller cage.

Cleaning Solvent-Based Materials

Follow the same procedure as for oil-based paint, but instead of paint thinner use the agent specified on the product label.

Cleaning Splashed Paint

No matter how careful you are, you will splash some paint onto windows, walkways, decks, and so forth. Remove it by scraping or by cleaning with the appropriate solvent.

Cleaning Finished Surfaces

Cleaning paint drips from finished surfaces can be difficult. If the finish is fully cured, the job is easier. However, you must act quickly, before the drip itself has a chance to cure. Give it a quick rub with a rag dampened in thinner. This may remove the drip without damaging the cured finish underneath. The stronger the cleaning agent, the more likely it is to dissolve the drip and the cured finish both.

If you get some of the wrong color paint on a freshly finished surface, there is no point in trying to remove it (unless it is still wet). The only solution is to paint over it with the right color.

Before you use solvent to remove paint from factory-finished products (such as windows, gutters, or siding), test it in an inconspicuous spot. If the solvent softens the factory finish, stop. Soap and water and a plastic scrubber may work.

Cleaning Porous Surfaces

It takes extra effort to remove splashed paint from porous materials, such as wood and concrete, without having the dirty cleaning agent soak into the surface. First, try to scrape off the bulk of the paint. Then scrub concrete with a wire brush and the appropriate agent. Paint drips on raw wood can be scraped or sanded out. Finish with several washes of fresh cleaning agent.

Blading Windows

To clean paint from window glass, use a razor blade. Many patent blade holders are available. The best approach is to cut the edge of the paint film with a matte knife or a utility knife at the line where the glazing meets the glass. Then use a razor scraper to lift the excess paint. Be careful not to cut into the glazing itself; new glazing is soft. Brush off any scrapings that cling to the window. Either drop off the area under the window or be prepared to pick up the mess.

Cleaning the Painter

You can wash latex paint off your skin fairly easily with soap and water. Getting it out

Blading Windows

1. Score the line where paint should end

Straightedge

Scored line

Utility knife

2. Scrape paint from glass, ending at the scored line

Scored line

Window scraper

of your hair can be more difficult. Mineral oil tends to dissolve both oil-based and latex paint, but it is itself hard to wash out. The best solution is to wear your hair tucked under a hat or scarf while you are painting, particularly when you are using a roller. A little petroleum jelly applied to your skin before painting will make cleanup easier. This is especially useful on eyelids and eyebrows.

You can clean off oil-based paint with thinner, but it will dry out your skin and hair. Instead, try a commercial hand cleaner that contains solvents strong enough to dissolve oil-based paint but that also contains lanolin or some other lubricants. It is not safe to use these products near your eyes. Prevent the paint from sticking to your eyelids by applying petroleum jelly before you roll

or spray. Cold cream can be used to dissolve paint around your eyes, but it takes forever.

Latex can be removed from fabric with soap and cold water, and oil-based paint can be removed with paint thinner. However, as a practical matter it is best to wear old clothes and just let them get painted.

Storing Paint and Solvents

Plan to keep some of each paint and finish that you use. You may need them for touch-ups or to match colors later. It is useful to have the labels of the original cans. This makes it easier to remember exactly what product was used where. However, a small amount of paint in a gallon can will dry out

quickly. If there is only a little paint left over, repackage it in a container just big enough to hold it. Paint stores often carry empty quart cans, but clean glass jars with tight-fitting lids are just as good. Be sure to label the paint clearly.

Reclaiming Used Thinner

Used thinner can be reclaimed to use in cleanup. This is especially easy if you are painting only on weekends; thinner will clear when it stands for a week. Use a funnel to transfer the used thinner back into a gasoline can, or a plastic bottle like the one in which it was sold. You can also use a glass jar or an empty gallon oil-based paint can (or a latex paint can, if it is thoroughly clean and dry). If you are using a glass jar, don't screw the lid down tight or

poke holes in the lid. Always leave room for vapor to escape.

When you start a cleaning session, decant the used thinner carefully to avoid stirring up the sediment at the bottom. Do not mix used thinner with new thinner.

Disposing of Paint

Environmental laws are different in each area. Check with your local sanitation department. They will explain the rules for disposing of paint and solvents in your community. In some places it is illegal to put these materials in the household garbage. You must take them to a waste disposal site or leave them to be picked up on special collection days.

If there are no local rules, you still should reclaim the thinners. Never pour thinner down a drain or a storm sewer, or even out on the ground. It will kill the plants, and the evaporating hydrocarbons damage the environment.

Excess paint can be poured on the ground a layer at a time and left to harden. Let each layer dry before you pour the next. When all the paint is hard, throw it out with the household garbage.

In most cases, the residue from reclaimed thinners can be left to dry. Then throw it in the garbage. Empty paint cans should be wiped out, left to dry, and then thrown away. Rags soaked with solvent or penetrating sealer should be left outside to dry. Heaped together, they are capable of spontaneous combustion. Let them dry thoroughly before you throw them out.

DDING FINISHING TOUCHES

Fashion experts say that it isn't the clothes that make the person; it's the accessories. This is also true in residential fashion, where the accessories are called the finishing touches. When the house is completely painted, the job is not quite completed, but the fun can begin. Look around the house for places to put personal statements.

Signage

Easy-to-read house numbers are a blessing to delivery people and visitors. Decide where they should go during the house inspection. If you don't like their present location, the numbers should be removed and the area behind them should be prepared for painting. Choose house numbers that fit the architectural style of the house. If you paint them, choose a color that stands out—perhaps a high-contrast pure hue.

Other signage—the family name, a crest, a historic building date—should also be treated consistent with the architectural style of the house.

Mailboxes

Curbside mailboxes are becoming an art form in many neighborhoods. They give you a chance to express your personality without spending a lot in time and materials. Some popular ideas are to build and paint the mailbox as a miniature version of the house; to paint it in all the colors of the house; and to apply special effects.

Do not ignore the mail slot. When you clean up, remove any drips and splashes from the cover. If the mail slot looks worn next to the freshly painted house, it may be time for a replacement.

Fences and Gates

Remember the fence when you develop the color scheme. Fences and gates that go with the house give the entire yard a coordinated look—and make the house look larger. The tops of fence posts and the fronts of gates are also good places to introduce a touch of whimsy or of elegance, whichever is appropriate to the house. Pick out these details in trim colors or add a special effect.

Furniture

Porch and patio furniture are also part of the house color scheme. Paint them to match the contrasting trim or in another coordinated color. Furniture must be painted for maintenance anyway, so why not do it when you do the house? Otherwise it will look shabby next to the new paint.

Don't Forget the Dog

Paint the doghouse, shed, and so forth to match the house. This is another way to give the yard a coordinated look. Remember that if these buildings are made of wood, they require the same preparation, painting, and maintenance as the house does. Because they are small, you can use them to work out the color scheme or to hone your painting skills. They also make good projects for children who would like to help paint.

Keep extra products on hand for touching up heavily used surfaces, such as this white picket fence and varnished front door.

Top left: Paint outdoor furniture in colors chosen to accent the house and yard. Use the same techniques as you would use for other metal surfaces.

Top right: Design the color scheme for outbuildings, such as this playhouse, to match the house design or choose a fanciful new scheme. An outbuilding is a good place to experiment with color combinations and painting techniques.

Bottom: Signage should be easy to find and easy to read. The red-accented numbers, furniture, and door on this yellow-and-white house really stand out.

INDEX

Proof-of-Purchase
0-89721-246-0

U.S./Metric Measure Conversion Chart

	Symbol	Formulas for Exact Measures — When you know:	Multiply by:	To find:	Rounded Measures for Quick Reference		
Mass (Weight)	oz	ounces	28.35	grams	1 oz		= 30 g
	lb	pounds	0.45	kilograms	4 oz		= 115 g
	g	grams	0.035	ounces	8 oz		= 225 g
	kg	kilograms	2.2	pounds	16 oz	= 1 lb	= 450 g
					32 oz	= 2 lb	= 900 g
					36 oz	= 2¼ lb	= 1000 g (1 kg)
Volume	tsp	teaspoons	5.0	milliliters	¼ tsp	= 1/24 oz	= 1 ml
	tbsp	tablespoons	15.0	milliliters	½ tsp	= 1/12 oz	= 2 ml
	fl oz	fluid ounces	29.57	milliliters	1 tsp	= 1/6 oz	= 5 ml
	c	cups	0.24	liters	1 tbsp	= ½ oz	= 15 ml
	pt	pints	0.47	liters	1 c	= 8 oz	= 250 ml
	qt	quarts	0.95	liters	2 c (1 pt)	= 16 oz	= 500 ml
	gal	gallons	3.785	liters	4 c (1 qt)	= 32 oz	= 1 liter
	ml	milliliters	0.034	fluid ounces	4 qt (1 gal)	= 128 oz	= 3¾ liter
Length	in.	inches	2.54	centimeters	3/8 in.	= 1 cm	
	ft	feet	30.48	centimeters	1 in.	= 2.5 cm	
	yd	yards	0.9144	meters	2 in.	= 5 cm	
	mi	miles	1.609	kilometers	2½ in.	= 6.5 cm	
	km	kilometers	0.621	miles	12 in. (1 ft)	= 30 cm	
	m	meters	1.094	yards	1 yd	= 90 cm	
	cm	centimeters	0.39	inches	100 ft	= 30 m	
					1 mi	= 1.6 km	
Temperature	° F	Fahrenheit	5/9 (after subtracting 32)	Celsius	32° F	= 0° C	
					68° F	= 20° C	
	° C	Celsius	9/5 (then add 32)	Fahrenheit	212° F	= 100° C	
Area	in.^{2}	square inches	6.452	square centimeters	1 in.^{2}	= 6.5 cm^2	
	ft^2	square feet	929.0	square centimeters	1 ft^2	= 930 cm^2	
	yd^2	square yards	8361.0	square centimeters	1 yd^2	= 8360 cm^2	
	a.	acres	0.4047	hectares	1 a.	= 4050 m^2	